The Merrill Studies
in
The American

Compiled by

William T. Stafford
Purdue University

Charles E. Merrill Publishing Company
A Bell & Howell Company
Columbus, Ohio

CHARLES E. MERRILL STUDIES

Under the General Editorship of
Matthew J. Bruccoli and Joseph Katz

Standard Book Number: 0-675-09268-X

Library of Congress Catalog Number: 71-136778

1 2 3 4 5 6 7 8 9 10—79 78 77 76 75 74 73 72 71

Printed in the United States of America

Preface

The American is in many ways the ideal introduction to the fiction of Henry James. Its early place in the James canon; its progenitive treatment of the international theme; its balanced blend of melodrama and comedy; its free and easy style; its memorable fabulistic protagonist, Christopher Newman; and—for our purposes here—the richly varied interpretative comment it has provoked (from James himself no less than others)—all make of it a peculiarly appropriate subject for this collection of critical studies which purport to recount something of its literary history during the almost one hundred years since it was first published.

I

Although in fact his third novel, James almost everywhere named *The American* his second, having virtually disavowed authorship of his first,[1] which was not published in book form until 1878, a full year following the first appearance in book form of *The American* in 1877. *Roderick Hudson* (1875) is the novel James usually named his first, and it, with *The American,* constitutes the duo with which all serious study of the Jamesian novel begins.

In still another context, however, James considered *The American* the "first" of his novels. In a letter late in life for a young writer who had inquired about how best one might begin reading James,[2] the

---

[1] The early *Watch and Ward* had appeared in serial form in the *Atlantic Monthly* as early as August-December, 1871; but James never reprinted it in any of his collected editions.

[2] The young writer was Stark Young. See *The Selected Letters of Henry James,* ed. by Leon Edel (New York: Farrar, Straus and Cudahy, 1955), pp. 108-109.

author supplied two lists of five novels each (both containing *The Wings of the Dove* and *The Golden Bowl*), but one beginning with *Roderick Hudson* and the other, with *The American*. The second list he described as "more 'advanced,'" containing as it does *The Tragic Muse* and *The Ambassadors* for *The Portrait of a Lady* and *The Princess Casamassima* of the first.

The American might well be considered more advanced than *Roderick Hudson* in any number of literal ways. The melodrama of its plotting, however, is probably not one of them. It is set in 1868, with Christopher Newman, a thirty-six-year-old, enormously rich American coming to Paris to discover, if he can, some splendid sequel to his achieved ability to make money. His plans are to "do" Europe and perhaps to find—in some supreme product of old-world civilization—the perfect wife. Through a Mrs. Tristram, the wife of an American acquaintance, Newman is introduced to Claire de Cintré, a young widow of noble birth, who strikes the American as precisely the woman he would like to marry. But on his first call at her home, he is turned away by her haughty elder brother, Urbain de Bellegarde.

But after a summer of traveling in Europe, Newman discovers that the Bellegardes are now willing to receive him; and he soon meets other members of the family: Urbain's wife; the charming younger brother Valentin; the shrewd and proud old Marquise, Madame de Bellegarde; and a servant, the sympathetic old Englishwoman, Mrs. Bread. The American becomes a close friend of Valentin, who encourages his courtship of his sister Claire. Urbain and his mother, however, tolerate him only because of his immense wealth. But Claire finally accepts his proposal, the engagement is formally announced, and the Marquis reluctantly introduces Newman to his aristocratic friends.

Meanwhile the American has come to know Mlle Noémie Nioche, a copyist of paintings, whose weak-willed, shabby-genteel father, becomes Newman's French teacher. Newman generously orders a number of Noémie's paintings in order to provide her a dowry, and he introduces her to Valentin, who immediately becomes infatuated. Soon thereafter Noémie gives up her painting, leaves her father's rooms, and becomes an apparently successful courtesan. Although Valentin clearly sees her for what she is, he continues to visit her.

Ultimately she is the cause of a duel in which the young Frenchman is fatally wounded. But before learning of the outcome of the duel, Newman is summoned by the Bellegardes and told that his marriage is off. Unwilling at the last moment to accept into the family a "commercial person," and hoping for a more aristocratic match with a Lord Deepmere, they had demanded that Claire break her engagement. And before Newman can confront her alone, he is called to young Valentin's death bed. Guessing what had happened, Valentin expresses his shame at his family's action and reveals to Newman that

Mrs. Bread knows a guilty secret about the family which the American may use to further his own ends.

After Valentin's funeral, Claire tells Newman of her decision to enter a convent. He thereupon seeks out Mrs. Bread and acquires from her proof that Madame de Bellegarde had murdered her husband. Newman threatens to expose the evidence, but Urbain and his mother still refuse to allow the marriage. Although determined at first to fulfill his revenge, Newman cannot bring himself to reveal the Bellegarde's secret. And when, after months of brooding and melancholy travel, he discovers that Claire had indeed taken the veil of a nun, he destroys the evidence of the murder.

Undeniably melodramatic though it be, the melodrama is decisively transformed by the novel's humor, its characterization of Newman, and its tone. The last quality in particular appears to have been catalytic. For James himself singled it out when, some thirty years later (1907), while writing the Preface for the novel's last revised edition, he said that what he had in fact been doing was "plotting arch-romance without knowing it." Moreover, he now viewed "with a certain sad envy . . . the free play of [what was then] so much unchallenged instinct." *The American* had all come to him, he wrote, "without intention, presumption, hesitation, [or] contrition"—resulting in an effect that was "equally undesigned and unabashed." This unbridled, instinctive quality, recognizable (I think) to almost any reader of the novel, is surely part of its free and easy charm and a considerable measure of its appeal.

The characterization of Newman adds to that same measure, as James himself clearly saw. His last word about *The American* was that it "must stand or fall by . . . [Newman's] more or less convincing image." Opinions, of course, vary about how convincing that image is. But probably few would deny the generic qualities in Newman's conception—generic to later and (mostly) greater protagonists in the James canon itself, and generic also to the idea of "the American" as many other native novelists were to render it.[3] More than a little of Christopher Newman is discernable in James's Caspar Goodwood, his Lambert Strether, his Adam Verver—later, if quite different, male

---

[3] Perhaps, even, to much later American scenario writers! Is Peter Fonda's Captain America, in Dennis Hopper's widely popular film of 1969, *Easy Rider,* radically different from Newman? Their names are clearly analogous. They both have made their fortune by questionable means. They both undertake quests to fulfill their dreams of a better life. They both confront established and intransigent societies which view them and their dreams as anathema. They both are at least indirectly involved with the deaths of members of that society (Valentin in the novel, the Southern lawyer in the film) who had been attracted to them. And both are themselves finally defeated by their own ambivalent limitations no less than by the rigidities of the two societies they affront.

characters affronting their destinies in Europe. But Newman is perhaps even more apparent in James's great female protagonists, his
heiresses of all the ages, his Daisy Miller, his Isabel Archer, his Milly
Theale. And common to all is the ambiguous conception in *The American* of a defeat (Newman does not, after all, get the girl) that may
as well be a conception of a renewal. "The negative imagination" that
Sallie Sears recently saw as most prominent in James's last novels,
"an unresolved debate about the promise and meaning of life, a debate
between a voice of yearning and a voice of restriction,"[4] has its clear,
unmistakable prologue in this early James novel. And *The American*
is more, not less important for its primary role in this Jamesian tradition. Thus, very early in James we see the inextricable tie between
possible moral growth, on the one hand, and initial limitation, some
innate capacity for renunciation, some almost pre-willed destiny to
failure on the other.

But the great, the unique appeal of Christopher Newman is the fun
he provides for the reader. Not quite anywhere else in James do we
find his particular charm: his free-wheeling grandness, his apparent
ease in the world, his larger-than-life self-reliance, from one perspective; his insensitivity, his awkwardness, his buffoonery, from another.
At least half of a different kind of fun results from the fact that
Newman, at first at any rate, pretty much sees himself as only those
who like him see him. The other half is perhaps that in the end he
is able to begin to see himself also as those who dislike him see him.
And the marvelously rich irony is all in between—the appealing charm
and the demonstrated limitation, an attractive innocence that may be
no more than a dull ignorance. Newman is quintessentially a comic
creation—but comic only in that very serious hyperbolic sense that
great comedy commands.

Designs and revelations of a different sort also appear in abundance
in the novel, harbingers of the emerging James canon no less than of
the modern novel itself as it was then developing on both sides of the
Atlantic. Gallic-American literary relations for example may well be
a central issue in the novel. American cultural history is undeniably
at play. And myth beyond the national is seen by some as a con-
tributing or controlling design. Studies of *The American* are thus rich
and various—and testimony enough to the sometime contradictory
ways the novel has come to be seen to have meaning, both by those
who have judged it successful and those who have judged it otherwise. Whatever the judgment, however, the collective studies themselves also constitute a kind of meaning; for the critical history of

---

[4] See her *The Negative Imagination: Form and Perspective in the Novels
of Henry James* (Ithaca: Cornell University Press, 1968).

any novel that has continued to live for a century is at least in part also the literary history of that same hundred years.

II

The first studies here collected on *The American* are those made by James himself: a brief comment from the *Notebooks* as James was looking back at the novel while considering the possibility of transforming it into a play; a spirited defense of the ending of the novel in a letter to William Dean Howells, editor of the *Atlantic Monthly* wherein the serial version appeared; and the magnificent Preface to the novel that James wrote for the selected New York Edition of his fiction in 1907. The Preface is clearly the major document here, not only in its record of James's recognition that the flaws in the novel did not necessarily negate its virtues (the instinctively easy flow of the narrative and the continuing appeal of Newman), but also, for its broader concerns with some theoretical aspects of the art of fiction. It is this Preface, to cite a single example, that contains James's classic distinction between the novel and the romance, between, that is, the real and the romantic—an issue much the concern of American novelists as early as Charles Brockden Brown and Hawthorne, even as it has been much the concern of such recent critics and literary historians of American fiction as Richard Chase and Leslie Fiedler.

A different kind of authorial comment is available to students of *The American* in the several revisions extant of this particular novel. The serial version first published in the *Atlantic Monthly* in 1876-1877 is not quite the version published by Osgood of Boston in book form in May of 1877, nor that of the English edition published by Macmillan in 1879, and certainly not that of the greatly revised version collected in the New York Edition of 1907. These revisions are an unusually rich source of information about James's developing artistry. And although variously used—and judged—as most of the studies in this collection demonstrate, few would question their unique contribution to an understanding of what James was attempting in his fiction. Also available, finally, is James's own dramatic version of this novel, his single play to have achieved at least a moderately successful run on the London stage, having lasted seventy performances between September 21 and December 3 of 1891.[5] The play, then, no less than the revisions should be considered with these other sources to get a comprehensive view of Jamesian comment on this novel.

---

[5] The text of the dramatic version of the novel is most readily available in *The Complete Plays of Henry James,* ed. by Leon Edel (Philadelphia: J. B. Lippincott Co., 1949).

The two contemporary reviews in the second section, one British, the other American, are capped with a brief retort to the latter simply to demonstrate the heated polarity of reaction *The American* was capable of provoking from the very beginning. James's letter to Howells balances nicely with it as indicative of another of the novel's aspects (the ending) that was to become increasingly controversial.

The next section extracts lengthy excerpts from three highly regarded book-length studies. Joseph Warren Beach's *The Method of Henry James* is a pioneer study, published only two years after James's death in 1916, and yet still the source from which all scholarly studies of James's method must begin. His concern here is with *The American* as James's "first large essay" on the international theme. Constance Rourke's *American Humor* first appeared in 1931, and hers is the initial study of Newman in the tradition of the stage Yankee, wherein "defeat had become at last an essential part of the national portraiture." Finally, in Oscar Cargill's *The Novels of Henry James,* we get a comprehensive study of the sources of the novel, some attention to the place of *The American* in the tradition of the international novel, and (in his copious notes) the most thorough coverage extant of critical and scholarly attention to the novel before 1961.

The two following essays work out elaborate "readings" of the novel in terms of special critical approaches. George Knox sees *The American* as "a fable, a fairly tale," a "cycle of trials en route to spiritual realization," all within the tradition of the American Romance, of which he sees James a rich part. John A. Clair, reading the text and the revisions with almost perverse closeness, inverts traditional interpretations, sees the "evil" Bellegardes with sympathy, the "good" Mrs. Bread as villainous, and thereby uncovers an exotic and novel plot of intrigue and blackmail.

The penultimate section consists of brief studies of *parts* of the novel. James W. Gargano, for example, discusses the opera-scene of Chapter Nineteen in terms of the foreshadowing function it performs. D. W. Jefferson sees a certain Jamesian "sense of type" represented in Mrs. Tristram. And Floyd C. Watkins and this writer, in the last two studies, reach contradictory conclusions about the virtues of early and late versions of the novel.

The final study in the collection, that by Cleanth Brooks, moves into a much larger context, comparing and contrasting Newman's American innocence to similar conceptions by two later American novelists, F. Scott Fitzgerald and William Faulkner. A final view of Newman in the company of Jay Gatsby and Thomas Sutpen is probably not an inappropriate final view to have.

WTS

Contents

4. Special Approaches

5. Special Achievements

6. The Context

1. From the Author

Henry James

From *The Notebooks*

—Reduced to its simplest expression . . . *The American* is the history of a plain man who is at the same time a fine fellow, who becomes engaged to the daughter of a patrician house, being accepted by her people on acct. of his wealth, and is then thrown over (by *them*) for a better match: after which he turns upon them to recover his betrothed (they have bullied her out of it), through the possession of a family secret which is disgraceful to them, dangerous to them, and which he holds over them as an instrument of compulsion and vengeance. They are frightened—they feel the screw: they dread exposure; but in the novel the daughter is already lost to the hero—she is swept away by the tragedy, takes refuge in a convent, breaks off her other threatened match, renounces the world, disappears. The hero, injured, out-raged, resentful, feels the strong temptation to *punish* the Belle-gardes, and for a day almost yields to it. Then he does the characteristically magnanimous thing—the characteristically good-natured thing—throws away his opportunity—lets them 'off'—lets them go.

From *The Notebooks of Henry James,* edited by F. O. Matthiessen and Kenneth B. Murdock (New York: Oxford University Press, 1947), p. 100. Copyright 1947 by Oxford University Press, Inc. Reprinted by permission.

From a Letter to William Dean Howells (March 30, 1877)

. . . I quite understand that as an editor you would go in for "cheerful endings"; but I am sorry that as a private reader you are not struck with the inevitability of the *American* ['s] dénouement. I fancied that most folks would feel that Mme. de Cintré couldn't, when the finish came, marry Mr. N[ewman]; and what the few persons who have spoken to me of the tale have expressed to me (e.g. Mrs. Kemble t'other day) was the fear that I should really put the marriage through. *Voyons;* it would have been impossible: they would have been an impossible couple, with an impossible problem before them. For instance—to speak very materially—where would they have lived? It was all very well for Newman to talk of giving her the whole world to choose from: but Asia and Africa being counted out, what would Europe and America have offered? Mme. de C. couldn't have lived in New York; depend upon it; and Newman, after his marriage (or rather *she,* after it) couldn't have dwelt in France. There would have been nothing left but a farm out West. No, the interest of the subject was, for me, (without my being at all a pessimist) its exemplification of one of those insuperable difficulties which present themselves in people's lives and from which the only issue is by forfeiture —by losing something. It was cruelly hard for poor N. to lose, certainly; but *que diable allait-il faire dans cette galère?* We are each the product of circumstances and there are tall stone walls which fatally divide us. I have written my story from Newman's side of the wall, and I understand so well how Mme. de Cintré couldn't really scramble over from *her* side! If I had represented her as doing so I should have made a prettier ending, certainly; but I should have felt as if I were throwing a rather vulgar sop to readers who don't really know the world and who don't measure the merit of a novel by its correspondence to the same. Such readers assuredly have a right to their entertainment, but I don't believe it is in me to give them, in a satisfactory way, what they require. . . .

Henry James

Preface to *The American*

"THE AMERICAN," which I had begun in Paris early in the winter of 1875–76, made its first appearance in "The Atlantic Monthly" in June of the latter year and continued there, from month to month, till May of the next. It started on its course while much was still unwritten, and there again come back to me, with this remembrance, the frequent hauntings and alarms of that comparatively early time; the habit of wondering what would happen if anything *should* "happen," if one should break one's arm by an accident or make a long illness or suffer, in body, mind, fortune, any other visitation involving a loss of time. The habit of apprehension became of course in some degree the habit of confidence that one would pull through, that, with opportunity enough, grave interruption never yet *had* descended, and that a special Providence, in short, despite the sad warning of Thackeray's "Denis Duval" and of Mrs. Gaskell's "Wives and Daughters" (that of Stevenson's "Weir of Hermiston" was yet to come) watches over

From *The Art of the Novel: Critical Prefaces by Henry James,* edited by R. P. Blackmur (New York: Charles Scribner's Sons, 1934), pp. 20-39. Copyright 1907 by Charles Scribner's Sons; renewal copyright 1935 by Henry James. Reprinted by permission of Charles Scribner's Sons.

anxious novelists condemned to the economy of serialisation. I make myself out in memory as having at least for many months and in many places given my Providence much to do: so great a variety of scenes of labour, implying all so much renewal of application, glimmer out of the books as I now read it over. And yet as the faded interest of the whole episode becomes again mildly vivid what I seem most to recover is, in its pale spectrality, a degree of joy, an eagerness on behalf of my recital, that must recklessly enough have overridden anxieties of every sort, including any view of inherent difficulties.

I seem to recall no other like connexion in which the case was met, to my measure, by so fond a complacency, in which my subject can have appeared so apt to take care of itself. I see now that I might all the while have taken much better care of it; yet, as I had at the time no sense of neglecting it, neither acute nor rueful solicitude, I can but speculate all vainly to-day on the oddity of my composure. I ask myself indeed if, possibly, recognising after I was launched the danger of an inordinate leak—since the ship has truly a hole in its side more than sufficient to have sunk it—I may not have managed, as a counsel of mere despair, to stop my ears against the noise of waters and *pretend* to myself I was afloat; being indubitably, in any case, at sea, with no harbour of refuge till the end of my serial voyage. If I succeeded at all in that emulation (in another sphere) of the pursued ostrich I must have succeeded altogether; must have buried my head in the sand and there found beatitude. The explanation of my enjoyment of it, no doubt, is that I was more than commonly enamoured of my idea, and that I believed it, so trusted, so imaginatively fostered, not less capable of limping to its goal on three feet than on one. The lameness might be what it would: I clearly, for myself, felt the thing *go*— which is the most a dramatist can ever ask of his drama; and I shall here accordingly indulge myself in speaking first of how, superficially, it did so proceed; explaining then what I mean by its practical dependence on a miracle.

It had come to me, this happy, halting view of an interesting case, abruptly enough, some years before: I recall sharply the felicity of the first glimpse, though I forget the accident of thought that produced it. I recall that I was seated in an American "horse-car" when I found myself, of a sudden, considering with enthusiasm, as the theme of a "story," the situation, in another country and an aristocratic society, of some robust but insidiously beguiled and betrayed, some cruelly wronged, compatriot: the point being in especial that he should suffer at the hands of persons pretending to represent the highest possible civilisation and to be of an order in every way superior to his own. What would he "do" in that predicament, how would he right himself, or how, failing a remedy, would he conduct himself under his wrong? This would be the question involved, and I remember well how, having entered the horse-car without a dream of it, I was presently to leave that vehicle in full possession of my answer. He would behave in the most interesting manner—it would all depend on that: stricken, smarting sore, he would arrive at his just vindication and then would fail of all triumphantly and all vulgarly enjoying it. He would hold his revenge and cherish it and feel its sweetness, and then in the very act of forcing it home would sacrifice it in disgust. He would let them go, in short, his haughty contemners, even while feeling them, with joy, in his power, and he would obey, in so doing, one of the large and easy impulses *generally* characteristic of his type. He wouldn't "forgive"—that would have, in the case, no application; he would simply turn, at the supreme moment, away, the bitterness of his personal loss yielding to the very force of his aversion. All he would have at the end would be therefore just the moral convenience, indeed the moral necessity, of his practical, but quite unappreciated, magnanimity; and one's last view of him would be that of a strong man indifferent to his strength and too wrapped in fine, too wrapped above all in *other* and intenser, reflexions for the assertion of his "rights." This last point was of the essence and constituted in fact the subject: there would be no subject at all, obviously,—or simply the commonest of the common,—if my gentleman should enjoy his advantage. I was charmed with my idea, which would take, however, much working out; and precisely because it had so much to give, I think, must I have dropped it for the time into the deep well of unconscious cerebration: not without the hope, doubtless, that it might eventually emerge from that reservoir, as one had already known the buried treasure to come to light, with a firm iridescent surface and a notable increase of weight.

This resurrection then took place in Paris, where I was at the moment living, and in December, 1875; my good fortune being apparently that Paris had ever so promptly offered me, and with an immediate directness at which I now marvel (since I had come back there, after earlier visitations, but a few weeks before), everything that was needed to make my conception concrete. I seem again at this distant day to see it become so quickly and

easily, quite as if filling itself with life in that air. The objectivity
it had wanted it promptly put on, and if the questions had been,
with the usual intensity, for my hero and his crisis—the whole
formidable list, the who? the what? the where? the when? the why?
the how?—they gathered their answers in the cold shadow of the
Arc de Triomphe, for fine reasons, very much as if they had been
plucking spring flowers for the weaving of a frolic garland. I saw
from one day to another my particular cluster of circumstances,
with the life of the splendid city playing up in it like a flashing
fountain in a marble basin. The very splendour seemed somehow
to witness and intervene; it was important for the effect of my
friend's discomfiture that it should take place on a high and lighted
stage, and that his original ambition, the project exposing him,
should have sprung from beautiful and noble suggestions—those
that, at certain hours and under certain impressions, we feel the
many-tinted medium by the Seine irresistibly to communicate. It
was all charmingly simple, this conception, and the current must
have gushed, full and clear, to my imagination, from the moment
Christopher Newman rose before me, on a perfect day of the divine
Paris spring, in the great gilded Salon Carré of the Louvre. Under
this strong contagion of the place he would, by the happiest of
hazards, meet his old comrade, now initiated and domiciled; after
which the rest would go of itself. If he was to be wronged he would
be wronged with just that conspicuity, with his felicity at just that
pitch and with the highest aggravation of the general effect of
misery mocked at. Great and gilded the whole trap set, in fine, for
his wary freshness and into which it would blunder upon its fate.
I have, I confess, no memory of a disturbing doubt; once the man
himself was imaged to me (and *that* germination is a process almost
always untraceable) he must have walked into the situation as
by taking a pass-key from his pocket.

But what then meanwhile would be the affront one would see
him as most feeling? The affront of course done him as a lover;
and yet not that done by his mistress herself, since injuries of this
order are the stalest stuff of romance. I was not to have him jilted,
any more than I was to have him successfully vindictive: both his
wrong and his right would have been in these cases of too vulgar a
type. I doubtless even then felt that the conception of Paris as the
consecrated scene of rash infatuations and bold bad treacheries
belongs, in the Anglo-Saxon imagination, to the infancy of art. The
right renovation of any such theme as *that* would place it in Boston
or at Cleveland, at Hartford or at Utica—give it some local con-

nexion in which we had not already had so much of it. No, I should
make my heroine herself, if heroine there was to be, an equal
victim—just as Romeo was not less the sport of fate for not having
been interestedly sacrified by Juliet; and to this end I had but to
imagine "great people" again, imagine my hero confronted and
involved with them, and impute to them, with a fine free hand,
the arrogance and cruelty, the tortuous behaviour, in given conditions, of which great people have been historically so often capable.
But as this was the light in which they were to show, so the essence
of the matter would be that he should at the right moment find
them in his power, and so the situation would reach its highest
interest with the question of his utilisation of that knowledge. It
would be here, in the possession and application of his power, that
he would come out strong and would so deeply appeal to our
sympathy. Here above all it really was, however, that my conception unfurled, with the best conscience in the world, the embla-
zoned flag of romance; which venerable ensign it had, though quite
unwittingly, from the first and at every point sported in perfect
good faith. I had been plotting arch-romance without knowing it,
just as I began to write it that December day without recognising
it and just as I all serenely and blissfully pursued the process from
month to month and from place to place; just as I now, in short,
reading the book over, find it yields me no interest and no reward
comparable to the fond perception of this truth.

The thing is consistently, consummately—and I would fain
really make bold to say charmingly—romantic; and all without
intention, presumption, hesitation, contrition. The effect is equally
undesigned and unabashed, and I lose myself at this late hour, I
am bound to add, in a certain sad envy of the free play of so much
unchallenged instinct. One would like to woo back such hours of
fine precipitation. They represent to the critical sense which the
exercise of one's *whole* faculty has, with time, so inevitably and so
thoroughly waked up, the happiest season of surrender to the invoked muse and the projected fable: the season of images so free
and confident and ready that they brush questions aside and dis-
port themselves, like the artless schoolboys of Gray's beautiful
Ode, in all the ecstasy of the ignorance attending them. The time
doubtless comes soon enough when questions, as I call them, rule
the roost and when the little victim, to adjust Gray's term again
to the creature of frolic fancy, doesn't dare propose a gambol till
they have all (like a board of trustees discussing a new outlay) sat
on the possibly scandalous case. I somehow feel, accordingly, that

it was lucky to have sacrificed on this particular altar while one still could; though it is perhaps droll—in a yet higher degree—to have done so not simply because one was guileless, but even quite under the conviction, in a general way, that, since no "rendering" of any object and no painting of any picture can take effect without some form of reference and control, so these guarantees could but reside in a high probity of observation. I must decidedly have supposed, all the while, that I was acutely observing—and with a blest absence of wonder at its being so easy. Let me certainly at present rejoice in that absence; for I ask myself how without it I could have written "The American."

Was it indeed meanwhile my excellent conscience that kept the charm as unbroken as it appears to me, in rich retrospect, to have remained?—or is it that I suffer the mere influence of remembered, of associated places and hours, all acute impressions, to palm itself off as the sign of a finer confidence than I could justly claim? It is a pleasure to perceive how again and again the shrunken depths of old work yet permit themselves to be sounded or—even if rather terrible the image—"dragged": the long pole of memory stirs and rummages the bottom, and we fish up such fragments and relics of the submerged life and the extinct consciousness as tempt us to piece them together. My windows looked into the Rue de Luxembourg—since then meagrely re-named Rue Cambon—and the particular light Parisian click of the small cab-horse on the clear asphalt, with its sharpness of detonation between the high houses, makes for the faded page to-day a sort of interlineation of sound. This sound rises to a martial clatter at the moment a troop of cuirassiers charges down the narrow street, each morning, to file, directly opposite my house, through the plain portal of the barracks occupying part of the vast domain attached in a rearward manner to one of the Ministères that front on the Place Vendôme; an expanse marked, along a considerable stretch of the street, by one of those high painted and administratively-placarded garden walls that form deep, vague, recurrent notes in the organic vastness of the city. I have but to re-read ten lines to recall my daily effort not to waste time in hanging over the window-bar for a sight of the cavalry the hard music of whose hoofs so directly and thrillingly appealed; an effort that inveterately failed—and a trivial circumstance now dignified, to my imagination, I may add, by the fact that the fruits of this weakness, the various items of the vivid picture, so constantly recaptured, must have been in themselves suggestive and inspiring, must have been rich strains, in their way, of the great Paris harmony. I have ever, in general, found it difficult to write of places under too immediate an impression—the impression that prevents standing off and allows neither space nor time for perspective. The image has had for the most part to be dim if the reflexion was to be, as is proper for a reflexion, both sharp and quiet: one has a horror, I think, artistically, of agitated reflexions.

Perhaps that is why the novel, after all, was to achieve, as it went on, no great—certainly no very direct—transfusion of the immense overhanging presence. It had to save as it could its own life, to keep tight hold of the tenuous silver thread, the one hope for which was that it shouldn't be tangled or clipped. This earnest grasp of the silver thread was doubtless an easier business in other places—though as I remount the stream of composition I see it faintly coloured again: with the bright protection of the Normandy coast (I worked away a few weeks at Étretat); with the stronger glow of southernmost France, breaking in during a stay at Bayonne; then with the fine historic and other "psychic" substance of Saint-Germain-en-Laye, a purple patch of terraced October before returning to Paris. There comes after that the memory of a last brief intense invocation of the enclosing scene, of the pious effort to unwind my tangle, with a firm hand, in the very light (that light of high, narrowish French windows in old rooms, the light somehow, as one always feels, of "style" itself) that had quickened my original vision. I was to pass over to London that autumn; which was a reason the more for considering the matter—the matter of Newman's final predicament—with due intensity: to let a loose end dangle over into alien air would so fix upon the whole, I strenuously felt, the dishonour of piecemeal composition. Therefore I strove to finish—first in a small dusky hotel of the Rive Gauche, where, though the windows again were high, the days were dim and the crepuscular court, domestic, intimate, "quaint," testified to ancient manners almost as if it had been that of Balzac's Maison Vauquer in "Le Père Goriot": and then once more in the Rue de Luxembourg, where a black-framed Empire portrait-medallion, suspended in the centre of each white panel of my almost noble old salon, made the coolest, discreetest, most measured decoration, and where, through casements open to the last mildness of the year, a belated Saint Martin's summer, the tale was taken up afresh by the charming light click and clatter, that sound as of the thin, quick, quite feminine surface-breathing of Paris, the shortest of rhythms for so huge an organism.

I shall not tell whether I did there bring my book to a close—and indeed I shrink, for myself, from putting the question to the test of memory. I follow it so far, the old urgent ingenious business, and then I lose sight of it: from which I infer—all exact recovery of the matter failing—that I did not in the event drag over the Channel a lengthening chain; which would have been detestable. I reduce to the absurd perhaps, however, by that small subjective issue, any undue measure of the interest of this insistent recovery of what I have called attendant facts. There always has been, for the valid work of art, a history—though mainly inviting, doubtless, but to the curious critic, for whom such things grow up and are formed very much in the manner of attaching young lives and characters, those conspicuous cases of happy development as to which evidence and anecdote are always in order. The development indeed must be certain to have been happy, the life sincere, the character fine: the work of art, to create or repay critical curiosity, must in short have been very "valid" indeed. Yet there is on the other hand no mathematical measure of that importance—it may be a matter of widely-varying appreciation; and I am willing to grant, assuredly, that this interest, in a given relation, will nowhere so effectually kindle as on the artist's own part. And I am afraid that after all even his best excuse for it must remain the highly personal plea—the joy of living over, as a chapter of experience, the particular intellectual adventure. Here lurks an immense homage to the general privilege of the artist, to that constructive, that creative passion—portentous words, but they are convenient—the exercise of which finds so many an occasion for appearing to him the highest of human fortunes, the rarest boon of the gods. He values it, all sublimely and perhaps a little fatuously, for itself—as the great extension, great beyond all others, of experience and of consciousness; with the toil and trouble a mere sun-cast shadow that falls, shifts and vanishes, the result of his living in so large a light. On the constant nameless felicity of this Robert Louis Stevenson has, in an admirable passage and as in so many other connexions, said the right word: that the partaker of the "life of art" who repines at the absence of the rewards, as they are called, of the pursuit might surely be better occupied. Much rather should he endlessly wonder at his not having to pay half his substance for his luxurious immersion. He enjoys it, so to speak, without a tax; the effort of labour involved, the torment of expression, of which we have heard in our time so much, being after all but the last refinement of his privilege. It may leave him weary and worn; but

how, after his fashion, he will have lived! As if one were to expect
at once freedom and ease! That silly safety is but the sign of
bondage and forfeiture. Who can imagine free selection—which is
the beautiful, terrible *whole* of art—without free difficulty? This
is the very franchise of the city and high ambition of the citizen.
The vision of the difficulty, as one looks back, bathes one's course
in a golden glow by which the very objects along the road are
transfigured and glorified; so that one exhibits them to other eyes
with an elation possibly presumptuous.

Since I accuse myself at all events of these complacencies I take
advantage of them to repeat that I value, in my retrospect, nothing
so much as the lively light on the romantic property of my subject
that I had not expected to encounter. If in "The American" I
invoked the romantic association without malice prepense, yet with
a production of the romantic effect that is for myself unmistake-
able, the occasion is of the best perhaps for penetrating a little the
obscurity of that principle. By what art or mystery, what craft of
selection, omission or commission, does a given picture of life
appear to us to surround its theme, its figures and images, with the
air of romance while another picture close beside it may affect us
as steeping the whole matter in the element of reality? It is a
question, no doubt, on the painter's part, very much more of
perceived effect, effect *after* the fact, than of conscious design—
though indeed I have ever failed to see how a coherent picture of
anything is producible save by a complex of fine measurements.
The cause of the deflexion, in one pronounced sense or the other,
must lie deep, however; so that for the most part we recognise the
character of our interest only after the particular magic, as I say,
has thoroughly operated—and then in truth but if we be a bit crit-
ically minded, if we find our pleasure, that is, in these intimate appreciations (for which, as I am well aware, ninety-nine readers in a
hundred have no use whatever). The determining condition would
at any rate seem so latent that one may well doubt if the full
artistic consciousness ever reaches it; leaving the matter thus a
case, ever, not of an author's plotting and planning and calculating,
but just of his feeling and seeing, of his conceiving, in a word, and
of his thereby inevitably expressing himself, under the influence
of one value or the other. These values represent different sorts
and degrees of the communicable thrill, and I doubt if any novelist,
for instance, ever proposed to commit himself to one kind or the
other with as little mitigation as we are sometimes able to find for
him. The interest is greatest—the interest of his genius, I mean,

and of his general wealth—when he commits himself in both directions; not quite at the same time or to the same effect, of course, but by some need of performing his whole possible revolution, by the law of some rich passion in him for extremes.

Of the men of largest responding imagination before the human scene, of Scott, of Balzac, even of the coarse, comprehensive, prodigious Zola, we feel, I think, that the deflexion toward either quarter has never taken place; that neither the nature of the man's faculty nor the nature of his experience has ever quite determined it. His current remains therefore extraordinarily rich and mixed, washing us successively with the warm wave of the near and familiar and the tonic shock, as may be, of the far and strange. (In making which opposition I suggest not that the strange and the far are at all necessarily romantic: they happen to be simply the unknown, which is quite a different matter. The real represents to my perception the things we cannot possibly *not* know, sooner or later, in one way or another; it being but one of the accidents of our hampered state, and one of the incidents of their quantity and number, that particular instances have not yet come our way. The romantic stands, on the other hand, for the things that, with all the facilities in the world, all the wealth and all the courage and all the wit and all the adventure, we never *can* directly know; the things that can reach us only through the beautiful circuit and subterfuge of our thought and our desire.) There have been, I gather, many definitions of romance, as a matter indispensably of boats, or of caravans, or of tigers, or of "historical characters," or of ghosts, or of forgers, or of detectives, or of beautiful wicked women, or of pistols and knives, but they appear for the most part reducible to the idea of the facing of danger, the acceptance of great risks for the fascination, the very love, of their uncertainty, the joy of success if possible and of battle in any case. This would be a fine formula if it bore examination; but it strikes me as weak and inadequate, as by no means covering the true ground and yet as landing us in strange confusions.

The panting pursuit of danger is the pursuit of life itself, in which danger awaits us possibly at every step and faces us at every turn; so that the dream of an intenser experience easily becomes rather some vision of a sublime security like that enjoyed on the flowery plains of heaven, where we may conceive ourselves proceeding in ecstasy from one prodigious phase and form of it to another. And if it be insisted that the measure of the type is then in the *appreciation* of danger—the sign of our projection of the

real being the smallness of its dangers, and that of our projection
of the romantic the hugeness, the mark of the distinction being in
short, as they say of collars and gloves and shoes, the size and
"number" of the danger—this discrimination again surely fails,
since it makes our difference not a difference of kind, which is
what we want, but a difference only of degree, and subject by that
condition to the indignity of a sliding scale and a shifting measure.
There are immense and flagrant dangers that are but sordid and
squalid ones, as we feel, tainting with their quality the very
defiances they provoke; while there are common and covert ones,
that "look like nothing" and that can be but inwardly and occultly
dealt with, which involve the sharpest hazards to life and honour
and the highest instant decisions and intrepidities of action. It is
an arbitrary stamp that keeps these latter prosaic and makes the
former heroic; and yet I should still less subscribe to a mere "subjective" division—I mean one that would place the difference
wholly in the temper of the imperilled agent. It would be impossible to have a more romantic temper than Flaubert's Madame
Bovary, and yet nothing less resembles a romance than the record
of her adventures. To classify it by that aspect—the definition of
the spirit that happens to animate her—is like settling the question
(as I have seen it witlessly settled) by the presence or absence of
"costume." Where again then does costume begin or end?—save
with the "run" of one or another sort of play? We must reserve
vague labels for artless mixtures.

The only *general* attribute of projected romance that I can see,
the only one that fits all its cases, is the fact of the kind of experience with which it deals—experience liberated, so to speak;
experience disengaged, disembroiled, disencumbered, exempt from
the conditions that we usually know to attach to it and, if we wish
so to put the matter, drag upon it, and operating in a medium
which relieves it, in a particular interest, of the inconvenience of a
related, a measurable state, a state subject to all our vulgar com-
munities. The greatest intensity may so be arrived at evidently—
when the sacrifice of community, of the "related" sides of situations, has not been too rash. It must to this end not flagrantly
betray itself; we must even be kept if possible, for our illusion,
from suspecting any sacrifice at all. The balloon of experience is
in fact of course tied to the earth, and under that necessity we
swing, thanks to a rope of remarkable length, in the more or less
commodious car of the imagination; but it is by the rope we know
where we are, and from the moment that cable is cut we are at

large and unrelated: we only swing apart from the globe—though remaining as exhilarated, naturally, as we like, especially when all goes well. The art of the romancer is, "for the fun of it," insidiously to cut the cable, to cut it without our detecting him. What I have recognised then in "The American," much to my surprise and after long years, is that the experience here represented is the disconnected and uncontrolled experience—uncontrolled by our general sense of "the way things happen"—which romance alone more or less successfully palms off on us. It is a case of Newman's own intimate experience all, that being my subject, the thread of which, from beginning to end, is not once exchanged, however momentarily, for any other thread; and the experience of others concerning us, and concerning him, only so far as it touches him and as he recognises, feels or divines it. There is our general sense of the way things happen—it abides with us indefeasibly, as readers of fiction, from the moment we demand that our fiction shall be intelligible; and there is our particular sense of the way they don't happen, which is liable to wake up unless reflexion and criticism, in us, have been skilfully and successfully drugged. There are drugs enough, clearly—it is all a question of applying them with tact; in which case the way things don't happen may be artfully made to pass for the way things do.

Amusing and even touching to me, I profess, at this time of day, the ingenuity (worthy, with whatever lapses, of a better cause) with which, on behalf of Newman's adventure, this hocus-pocus is attempted: the value of the instance not being diminished either, surely, by its having been attempted in such evident good faith. Yes, all is romantic to my actual vision here, and not least so, I hasten to add, the fabulous felicity of my candour. The way things happen is frankly not the way in which they are represented as having happened, in Paris, to my hero: the situation I had conceived only saddled me with that for want of my invention of something better. The great house of Bellegarde, in a word, would, I now feel, given the circumstances, given the *whole* of the ground, have comported itself in a manner as different as possible from the manner to which my narrative commits it; of which truth, moreover, I am by no means sure that, in spite of what I have called my serenity, I had not all the while an uneasy suspicion. I had dug in my path, alas, a hole into which I was destined to fall. I was so possessed of my idea that Newman should be ill-used— which was the essence of my subject—that I attached too scant an importance to its fashion of coming about. Almost any fashion would serve, I appear to have assumed, that would give me my main chance for him; a matter depending not so much on the particular trick played him as on the interesting face presented by him to *any* damnable trick. So where I part company with *terra-firma* is in making that projected, that performed outrage so much more showy, dramatically speaking, than sound. Had I patched it up to a greater apparent soundness my own trick, artistically speaking, would have been played; I should have cut the cable without my reader's suspecting it. I doubtless at the time, I repeat, believed I had taken my precautions; but truly they should have been greater, to impart the air of truth to the attitude—that is first to the pomp and circumstance, and second to the queer falsity —of the Bellegardes.

They would positively have jumped then, the Bellegardes, at my rich and easy American, and not have "minded" in the least any drawback—especially as, after all, given the pleasant palette from which I have painted him, there were few drawbacks to mind. My subject imposed on me a group of closely-allied persons animated by immense pretensions—which was all very well, which might be full of the promise of interest: only of interest felt most of all in the light of comedy and of irony. This, better understood, would have dwelt in the idea not in the least of their not finding Newman good enough for their alliance and thence being ready to sacrifice him, but in that of their taking with alacrity everything he could give them, only asking for more and more, and then adjusting their pretensions and their pride to it with all the comfort in life. Such accommodation of the theory of a noble indifference to the practice of a deep avidity is the real note of policy in forlorn aristocracies—and I meant of course that the Bellegardes should be virtually forlorn. The perversion of truth is by no means, I think, in the displayed acuteness of their remembrance of "who" and "what" they are, or at any rate take themselves for; since it is the misfortune of all insistence on "worldly" advantages—and the situation of such people bristles at the best (by which I mean under whatever invocation of a superficial simplicity) with emphasis, accent, assumption—to produce at times an effect of grossness. The picture of their tergiversation, at all events, however it may originally have seemed to me to hang together, has taken on this rococo appearance precisely because their preferred course, a thousand times preferred, would have been to haul him and his fortune into their boat under cover of night perhaps, in any case as quietly and with as little bumping and splashing as possible, and there accommodate him with the very safest and most convenient seat. Given Newman, given the fact that the thing constitutes itself organically as *his* adventure, that too might very well be a situation and a subject: only it wouldn't have been the theme of "The American" as the book stands, the theme to which I was from so early pledged. Since I had wanted a "wrong" this other turn might even have been arranged to give me *that*, might even have been arranged to meet my requirement that somebody or something should be "in his power" so delightfully; and with the signal effect, after all, of "defining" everything. (It is as difficult, I said above, to trace the dividing-line between the real and the romantic as to plant a milestone between north and south; but I am not sure an infallible sign of the latter is not this rank vegetation of the "power" of bad people that good get into, or *vice versa*. It is so rarely, alas, into *our* power that any one gets!)

It is difficult for me to-day to believe that I had not, as my work went on, *some* shade of the rueful sense of my affront to verisimilitude; yet I catch the memory at least of no great sharpness, no true critical anguish, of remorse: an anomaly the reason of which in fact now glimmers interestingly out. My concern, as I saw it, was to make and to keep Newman consistent; the picture of his consistency was all my undertaking, and the memory of *that* infatuation perfectly abides with me. He was to be the lighted figure, the others—even doubtless to an excessive degree the woman who is made the agent of his discomfiture—were to be the obscured; by which I should largely get the very effect most to be invoked, that of a generous nature engaged with forces, with difficulties and dangers, that it but half understands. If Newman was attaching enough, I must have argued, his tangle would be sensible enough; for the interest of everything is all that it is *his* vision, *his* conception, *his* interpretation: at the window of his wide, quite sufficiently wide, consciousness we are seated, from that admirable position we "assist." He therefore supremely matters; all the rest matters only as he feels it, treats it, meets it. A beautiful infatuation this, always, I think, the intensity of the creative effort to get into the skin of the creature; the act of personal possession of one being by another at its completest—and with the high enhancement, ever, that it is, by the same stroke, the effort of the artist to preserve for his subject that unity, and for his use of it (in other words for the interest he desires to excite) that effect of a *centre*, which most economise its value. Its value is most discussable when that economy has most operated; the content and the "importance" of a work of art are in fine wholly dependent on its *being* one: outside of which all prate of its representative character, its meaning and its bearing, its morality and humanity, are an impudent thing. Strong in that character, which is the condition of its really bearing witness at all, it is strong every way. So much remains true then on behalf of my instinct of multiplying the fine touches by which Newman should live and communicate life; and yet I still ask myself, I confess, what I can have made of "life," in my picture, at such a juncture as the interval offered as elapsing between my hero's first accepted state and the nuptial rites that are to crown it. Nothing here is in truth "offered"—everything is evaded, and the effect of this, I recognise, is of the oddest. His relation to Madame de Cintré takes a great stride, but the author appears to view that but as a signal for letting it severely alone.

I have been stupefied, in so thoroughly revising the book, to find, on turning a page, that the light in which he is presented immediately after Madame de Bellegarde has conspicuously introduced him to all her circle as her daughter's husband-to-be is, that of an evening at the opera quite alone; as if he wouldn't surely spend his leisure, and especially those hours of it, with his intended. Instinctively, from that moment, one would have seen them intimately and, for one's interest, beautifully together; with some illustration of the beauty incumbent on the author. The truth was that at this point the author, all gracelessly, could but hold his breath and pass; lingering was too difficult—he had made for himself a crushing complication. Since Madame de Cintré was after all to "back out" every touch in the picture of her apparent loyalty would add to her eventual shame. She had acted in clear good faith, but how could I give the *detail* of an attitude, on her part, of which the foundation was yet so weak? I preferred, as the minor evil, to shirk the attempt—at the cost evidently of a signal loss of "charm"; and with this lady, altogether, I recognise, a light plank, too light a plank, is laid for the reader over a dark "psychological" abyss. The delicate clue to her conduct is never definitely placed in his hand: I must have liked verily to think it *was* delicate and to flatter myself it was to be felt with finger-tips rather than heavily tugged at. Here then, at any rate, is the romantic *tout craché*—the fine flower of Newman's experience blooming in a medium "cut off" and shut up to itself. I don't for a moment pronounce any spell proceeding from it necessarily the less workable, to a rejoicing ingenuity, for that; beguile the reader's suspicion of *his* being shut up, transform it for *him* into a positive illusion of the largest liberty, and the success will ever be proportionate to the chance. Only all this gave me, I make out, a great deal to look to, and I was perhaps wrong in thinking that Newman by himself, and for any occasional extra inch or so I might smuggle into his measurements, would see me through my wood. Anything more liberated and disconnected, to repeat my terms, than his prompt general profession, before the Tristrams, of aspiring to a "great" marriage, for example, could surely not well be imagined. I had to take that over with the rest of him and fit it in—I had indeed to exclude the outer air. Still, I find on re-perusal that I have been able to breathe at least in my aching void; so that, clinging to my hero as to a tall, protective, good-natured elder brother in a rough place, I leave the record to stand or fall by his more or less convincing image.

2. From the Reviews

George Saintsbury

A Review of *The American*

We have but one thing against Mr. James, and we wish we could say as much for most of the novelists whose work comes before us. He has read Balzac, if it be possible, just a little too much; has read him until he has fallen into the one sin of his great master, the tendency to bestow refined dissection and analysis on characters which are not of sufficient intrinsic interest to deserve such treatment. No doubt this is a fault which savours of virtue; but still it is a fault, and a fault which renders it extremely difficult to fix one's attention on *The American* until the excellence of Mr. James's manipulation fairly forces one for very shame to interest oneself in his story. The hero and heroine are the chief stumbling-blocks. He is a typical Yankee who, after serving with distinction in the civil war, has set to work at making a fortune, and has made it by the help of things in general—washtubs, soap, and oil being more particularly specified. He comes naturally to Paris to spend the fortune, and to look out for something exceedingly superior in wives. Unfortunately for himself, he has proposed to him a certain Countess de Cintré, an angel in herself, but appertaining to a by

From *Academy,* XII (July, 1877), 33.

no means angelic family, who represent in race and character the stiffest types both of English and French nobility. They, of course, cannot do away with the washtubs, even though transmuted into dollars, and by working on Mme de Cintré's filial ideas they at last succeed in getting the match broken off. There are several minor characters who are decidedly better than the principals. Such are the old Marquise, who bears, however, a rather perilous likeness to Lady Kew; her younger son, a capital fellow and a partisan of the ill-treated Yankee; a match-making and platonically flirtatious American matron, and others. Also we have a ghastly family secret, a fatal duel, and a retirement to a convent; so that Mr. James has been by no means stingy of what some people will regard as the solids of his feast. But we wish we could like his chief figures. The portrait of his countryman must of course be taken as accurate, and is evidently sympathetic. But if not only the *naïf* consciousness and avowal of being as good as anybody else, but also the inability to understand how the anybody else may possibly differ from him on this point, be taken from life, the defect of repulsion strikes us as a serious one. There is, moreover, something exceedingly jarring to our possibly effete nerves in the idea of a man who seriously entertains the idea of revenging himself for a personal slight by making use of a family secret which he has surreptitiously got hold of. It is true he does not do it, but he threatens to do so, and tries to make profit of the threat. After this we cannot help feeling on the side of his enemies, scoundrels as they are. And the lady, though her temperament and French ideas of duty explain her conduct not insufficiently, is far too shadowy and colourless. The book is an odd one, for, though we cannot call it a good book, there is no doubt whatever that it is worth a score of the books which we are wont truly enough in a sense to call good.

Anonymous

A Review of *The American*

—The *Atlantic* for January contains a number of good things and some poor ones. Mr. James's story, "The American," which has now reached its eighteenth chapter, has gradually become the familiar feature of the magazine, for which most of its readers from month to month grow impatient, and it is a story which certainly gets more interesting as it goes on. We confess to having had at first a feeling of irritation at being called upon to take an interest in a specimen of a type which, as a type, is, to say the least, not æsthetically attractive. The self-made American, who has suddenly grown rich by "operations" of one kind or another, and has taken himself and his wealth to Europe, is a familiar enough character in literature, but usually the character has been made a comic one, and we have been called upon to laugh at the ridiculous figure cut by our compatriot in the gilded saloons of the effete but critical Europeans, or at his shocking display of ignorance and barbarism as he wanders through "specimen ruins" and "specimen galleries." Mr. James, however, has placed before himself a very different task. He has undertaken to make use of this same type as a serious

From *The Nation*, January 11, 1877, p. 29.

27

character in a love story. Newman, as we understand him, is a man who by means of a God-given talent for making money has, while still a young man, accumulated a great fortune (we confess to a sneaking curiosity as to which side of the market he operated upon), and while being in externals an entirely untrained and unsophisticated person, is possessed of that tact and adaptability to circumstances and refinement of mind which have always been set down as distinguishingly American traits by such unbiassed observers as the English. This man is now taken to France, made to fall in love with a charming French widow, of a family as old and blue-blooded as any in France, filled with and living on the pride of ancestry, ignorant of any world but their own, and looking down with sovereign contempt upon all persons "in trade." It is in this atmosphere of perfectly cold politeness and perfect inanity that our American barbarian lover has to appear to advantage, and to interest the reader. That he does so at all is a striking proof of Mr. James's power as a novelist, and he unquestionably does so a great deal. Of the story as a whole it would be rash to express an opinion till it is completed; but it is safe to say that it is by far the most important contribution to American fiction made for a long time.

Anonymous

A Retort to a Review of
The American

—In reading lately, in The Nation, some remote praise of Mr. James's story of The American by a critic who "confessed to having had at first a feeling of irritation at being called upon to take an interest in a specimen of a type which, as a type, was to say the least not æsthetically attractive," I felt a concern which I wish to express for the condition of a mind so febrile in its sensitiveness as to be shocked at the bare thought of a type like Newman being introduced into a novel, as hero. I at once perceived how greatly this select being must have to limit his reading of fiction, in order to retain any nervous system whatever. Such a story as Le Père Goriot, or César Birotteau, for example, would not simply subject him to "nervous irritation" at the start, but must prostrate him for days. Freytag's Soll und Haben would be very damaging to him. Adam Bede. Silas Marner, and Alton Locke should be kept under lock and key wherever there is danger of this gentleman's accidentally getting hold of them. I do not quite like to think of

From *The Atlantic Monthly*, XXXIX (March, 1877), 368.

the consequences of his coming in contact with Thackeray's Hog-garty Diamond; and there are people so common in Shakespeare's plays that I am sure those dramas cannot be pleasant reading to The Nation's critic. How does he manage with Sancho Panza, or Gil Blas? So superior a critic is cut off from the great variety of fiction in which ruder readers take delight. For instance, in a case like Reade's Love Me Little, Love Me Long, the lover, Dodd, is not a whit more æsthetic than the lover, Newman, in Mr. James's American. A devout admirer of The Nation, however, tells me we should be glad that a person of such nice discrimination has not long before this perished through suffering from vulgar types in literature. I should like to believe that the case is not so bad as it seems, and that this critic appears more precariously situated than he is, simply because he has allowed himself to talk rubbish.

3. From Book-Length Studies

Joseph Warren Beach

From *The Method of Henry James*

"The American" is the first large essay of James in treatment of the theme that was to occupy so much of his attention all along, —the contrast of the American and the European cultures. And it remains to this day an effective piece of work. The self-made American without antecedents and traditions brought in contrast with a group of persons for whom these are almost the whole of life; the man of strong and unlimited self-reliance in contrast to men and women hedged and thwarted in every direction by the restraints of family and caste—the simple, straightforward, easy-going westerner in his dealings with these formal, sophisticated, inordinately polite and treacherous people; it makes a story and a spectacle of endless richness and variety. The idea is clearly conceived, and there is no detail of the story that it does not inform and make relevant. The sub-plot of Valentin de Bellegarde and Noémie Nioche is obviously introduced for the purpose of illustrating certain aspects of the social contrast which do not come out in Newman's own love affair. The friendship of Valentin and Christopher is a delightful case of the mutual attraction of opposites. "No two parties to an alliance could have come to it from a wider separation, but it was what each brought out of the queer dim distance that formed the odd attraction for the other."[1]

The social contrast comes out most strikingly, however, and certainly to our greatest amusement, in the series of scenes in which the blunt and humorous westerner is opposed to the frigid courtliness of the elder Bellegardes, above all on those occasions when, having accepted him as a suitor for the hand of Claire, they yet endeavor, largely without success, to make him understand the enormous condescension in their friendly treatment of a "commercial" person. The American millionaire, conscious of his own power and his own good character, can be made to appreciate but dimly the social inferiority imputed to him. He does feel keenly, however, if somewhat obscurely, the quality of culture displayed in the manners of his French friends. He feels it naturally most of all in the style of the woman he loves. "She gave him, the charming woman, the sense of an elaborate education, of her having passed through mysterious ceremonies and processes of culture, of her having been fashioned and made flexible to certain deep social needs. All this . . . made her seem rare and precious—a very expensive article."[2] Her rank made of Claire de Cintré "a kind of historical formation." Rank was something which heretofore he had heard attributed only to military personages. He now appreciated the attribution of rank to women. "The designations representing it in France struck him as ever so pretty and becoming, with a property in the bearer, this particular one, that might match them and make a sense—something fair and softly bright, that had motions of extraordinary lightness and indeed a whole new and unfamiliar play of emphasis and pressure, a new way, that is, of not insisting and not even, as one might think, wanting or knowing, yet all to the effect of attracting and pleasing."[3] But even the odious relatives of Claire and the gentry gathered together by them at their ball share this quality of rank, and something of the finish and beauty of style entailed in their being likewise "historical formations." And we may say in passing that the American himself does not come out at all badly in the comparison. His manners,

---

[1] Vol. II, p. 139.
[2] Vol. II, p. 165.
[3] Id., p. 122.

while not the least bit historical, have a freedom and candor, a largeness and natural breeding, which make you prefer them to the article more expensively produced.

It is an effective piece of work. . . . And it is very much in the early manner. I will not dwell on the superficial points of technique in which it resembles "Roderick Hudson." The dialogue is often very good; but not at all in the way the dialogue is good in "The Awkward Age." It is refreshing to have the hero "bet his life on" something, or to have him urge an amused Parisian to "give" somebody "one in the eye." There are passages of talk, however, which have somewhat lost their savor. We cannot help feeling at times that Valentin and even his sister are permitted to show themselves younger and less practiced hands than the author intended. And we are conscious of a certain perfunctory character in most of Newman's exemplary love-making.

But the early manner is exhibited in ways more important than these. It resides essentially in what we may call the greater objectivity of the work. The chief concern of the author seems to be for the scenical effectiveness of what is said and done. In the later work the scene is used chiefly in order to objectify the idea. Here the idea is the opportunity for scene. The characters express themselves more violently here, in word and gesture. This emotional emphasis reaches its culmination in the chapter in which Claire announces her intention of becoming a nun. In this one chapter[4] we read that "Newman gave a great rap on the floor with his stick and a long grim laugh"; that "he struck his heart and became more eloquent than he knew"; that he "almost shouted"; "he glared as if at her drowning beyond help, then he broke out"; "he clasped his hands and began to tremble visibly"; "he dropped into a chair and sat looking at her with a long inarticulate wail"; "he sprang to his feet in loud derision." Nowhere else in James, I think, is there such a lavish use of irony as that indulged in by Newman and the grim Marquise. Their remarks are as good as lines in a smart play. And that is the point. These scenes in which new world and old world are pitted against one another are introduced for their theatrical effectiveness, like certain brilliant scenes in Thackeray or in Dumas *père*. Such is the scene in which the Marquis is obliged to introduce to all his *monde* the "commercial" person who is going to marry his sister. Such is the scene in the Parc Monceau in which Newman announces to the Marquis and

---

[4] Chap. xx.

the old Marquise his possession of the incriminating paper. It makes a fine show, the bravery with which his adversaries, deep-stricken as they are, bear up in the face of the world,—their display of that "very superior style of brazen assurance, of what M. Nioche called *l'usage du monde* and Mrs. Tristram called the grand manner."[5] This is not incompatible with a suppressed but terrible exhibition of passion. Upon one of Newman's ironic sallies on this occasion, "the Marquis gave a hiss that fairly evoked for our friend some vision of a hunched back, an erect tail and a pair of shining evil eyes. 'I demand of you to step out of our path!' "[6] That is good "business," and a good line. But the best line of all is that of the Marquis in the scene where Newman has informed him and his mother of Valentin's death-bed apology for their conduct. He had apologized for the conduct of his own mother! "For a moment the effect of these words was as if he had struck a physical blow. A quick flush leaped into the charged faces before him—it was like a jolt of full glasses, making them spill their wine. Urbain uttered two words which Newman but half heard, but of which the aftersense came to him in the reverberation of the sound. '*Le misérable!*' "[7]

The point of view is throughout chiefly that of Newman. But not the same use is made of this as would have been made in a later book. We see what Newman sees, but he does not interpret it to us. The author interprets it, and he is sometimes obliged—in order to get Newman into the picture—to give us a glimpse or two beyond what Newman sees. "We have noted him as observant," says James in the scene when the Marquise is forced to invite Newman to a ball at *her* house; "yet on this occasion he failed to catch a thin sharp eyebeam, as cold as a flash of steel, which passed between Madame de Bellegarde and the Marquis, and which we may presume to have been a commentary on the innocence displayed in that latter clause of this speech."[8] That latter clause had been a statement that "it mattered very little whether he met his friends at her house or his own." This showed how little he understood of the ways of thought of those with whom he was dealing. All along he showed surprising unconsciousness of the pitfalls amid which he was walking. All along he was very largely unaware of the comedy in which he was playing his part. It was in

---

[5] P. 496.
[6] P. 489.
[7] P. 431.
[8] P. 285.

vain, for example, that Valentin tried to make him understand what was involved in the condescension of Urbain and his mother. And when he refrained from explanations, Christopher had no idea what that cost him. "I know not," says the author, "whether in renouncing the mysterious opportunity to which he alluded Valentin felt himself do something very generous. If so he was not rewarded; his generosity was not appreciated. Newman failed to recognize any power to disconcert or to wound him, and he had now no sense of coming off easily."[9]

A story in which the main actor is so uninitiated can bear no very close resemblance to the story of Isabel Archer or Fleda Vetch or Lambert Strether. There is here no revelation of anything through Newman's consciousness—nothing that depends on his *understanding*. There is in fact no spiritual dilemma. That is why the book is not among the greatest of its author's. There is a gallant fight for a woman. There is an amusing and finally tragic social contrast in which the American hero is one of the terms. And that is the main point in which this is recognizable as a novel of Henry James.

---

[9] P. 160.

Constance Rourke

From *American Humor: A Study of the National Character*

Even the title was a fulfillment. Who ever heard of a significant English novel called *The Englishman* or an excellent French novel called *Le Français?* The simple and aggressive stress belonged to an imagination perennially engaged by the problem of the national type. The name Newman had significance, faintly partaking of that comic symbolism by which a hero in one of the Yankee fables was called Jedidiah Homebred.

At the opening of the story, as Newman strolled through the Salon Carré examining masterpieces, James declared that no one with an eye for types could have failed to perceive that he was an American. "Indeed such an observer might have made an ironic point of the almost ideal completeness with which he filled out the mold of race. . . . He had the flat jaw and firm, dry neck which are frequent in the American type. . . . Long, lean, and muscular, he suggested an intensity of unconscious resistance. . . . His usual attitude and carriage had a liberal looseness; but when, under a special intensity of inspiration, he straightened himself, he looked like a grenadier on parade." Newman was of the familiar build; he had the familiar consciousness of costume; in an ensuing scene he appeared in a blue satin cravat of too light a shade and with a shirt front obtrusively wide. But according to James it was the eye, of a clear cold gray, that told the final story: "an eye in which the unacquainted and the expert were singularly blended"—the innocent and the shrewd. "I can't make you out," said Mrs. Tristram, "whether you are very simple or very deep."

Newman's local origin was never given; though he stemmed from the Yankee, he was not of New England, certainly not of Boston. The Pacific Coast had been the scene of his financial successes; and there were fixed as occuring before 1868, that is, during the period of the gold rush. He might have been in San Francisco or Virginia City with Mark Twain; he had habits of the time and place. "He had sat with western humorists in circles around cast-iron stoves and had seen tall stories grow taller without toppling over, and his imagination had learnt the trick of building straight and high." Young Madame de Bellegarde said that if she had not known who Newman was she could have taken him for a duke—an American duke, the Duke of California. "The way you cover ground!" said Valentin de Bellegarde. "However, being as you are a giant, you move naturally in seven league boots. . . . You're a man of the world to a livelier tune than ours."

Fabulous stories were told about Newman. At the great ball given by the Bellegardes he was presented to the Duchess, whose nodding tiara and triple chins and vast expanse of bosom troubled him, and who looked at him "with eyes that twinkled like a pair of polished pin-heads in a cushion." "With her little circle of admirers this remarkable woman reminded him of a Fat Lady at a fair." "I've heard all sorts of extraordinary things about you," she said, fixing her small unwinking gaze upon him. "*Voyons*, are they true? . . . Oh, you've had your *légende*. You've had a career of the most chequered, the most *bizarre*. What's that about your having founded a city some ten years ago in the great West, a city which contains today half a million inhabitants? Isn't it half a million, messieurs? You're exclusive proprietor of the wonderful place and are consequently fabulously rich, and you'd be richer still if you didn't grant lands and houses free of rent to all newcomers who'll pledge themselves never to smoke cigars. At this game, in three years, we're told, you're going to become President of all the Americas."

"He liked doing things that involved his paying for people," said James; "the vulgar truth is he enjoyed 'treating' them. . . . Just as it was a gratification to him to be nobly dressed, just so it was a private satisfaction (for he kept the full flavor of it quite delicately to himself) to see people occupied and amused at his pecuniary expense and by his profuse interposition. To set a large body of them in motion and transport them to a distance, to have special conveyances, to charter railway-carriages and steamboats, harmonized with his relish for bold processes and made hospitality the potent thing it should ideally be."

Newman preserved a negligent air in such enterprises just as he casually gave an order for copies of half a dozen masterpieces to Mademoiselle Noémie in order to provide money for her *dot*. But he clearly saw the direction of Mademoiselle Noémie's purpose when she announced to him that her paintings were daubs in the hope that her candor might bring her a more considerable profit. He passed over her declaration with his customary blankness, dropping into some hidden cavern of his mind the revelation that his taste had been at fault. "You've got something it worries me to have missed," said Valentin. "It's not money, it's not even brains, though evidently yours have been excellent for your purpose. It's not your superfluous stature, though I should have rather liked to be a couple of inches taller. It's a sort of air you have of being imperturbably, being irremovably and indestructibly (that's the thing) at home in the world. When I was a boy my father assured me it was by just such an air that people recognized a Bellegarde. He called my attention to it. He didn't advise me to cultivate it; he said that as we grew up it always came of itself. . . . But you who, as I understand it, have made and sold articles of vulgar household use—you strike me—in a fashion of your own, as a man who stands about at his ease and looks straight over ever so many high walls. I seem to see you move everywhere like a big stockholder on his favorite railroad. You make me feel awfully my want of shares. And yet the world used to be supposed to be ours. What is it I miss?"

Newman's reply was resounding, and might have been taken out of many an American oration of the past. "It's the proud consciousness of honest toil, of having produced something yourself that somebody has been willing to pay for—since that's the definite measure. Since you speak of my washtubs—which were lovely—

isn't it just they and their loveliness that make up my good conscience?"

"Oh, no; I've seen men who had gone beyond washtubs, who had made mountains of soap—strong-smelling yellow soap, in great bars; and they've left me perfectly cold."

"Then it's just the regular treat of being an American citizen," said Newman. "That sets a man right up."

The tone, as one knows Newman, was jocose, with an admixture of serious conviction. It was the comic belligerent tone that had spread through the assertive nationalism of the Yankee fables; and James seemed to enjoy the mixed quality. He glossed over nothing, writing with gusto of Newman's early preoccupation with money, which had also been dominant in Yankee swapping and bargaining. He admitted that his hero considered "what he had been placed in the world for was . . . simply to gouge a fortune, the bigger the better, out of its hard material. This idea completely filled his horizon and contented his imagination. Upon the uses of money, upon what one might do with a life into which one had succeeded in injecting the golden stream, he had up to the eve of his fortieth year very scantly reflected."

"I cared for money-making, but I have never cared so very terribly about money," Newman told Madame de Cintré with expansive confidence, launching into self-revelation. As he sat in her drawing-room he stretched his legs; his questions had a simple ease. "Don't you find it rather lifeless here," he inquired, "so far from the street?" "Your house is tremendously old then?" he asked a little later. When Valentin had found the date, 1627, over the mantelpiece, Newman announced roundly, "Your house is of a very fine style of architecture." "Are you interested in questions of architecture?" asked Valentin. "Well, I took the trouble this summer to examine—as well as I can calculate—some four hundred and seventy churches. Do you call that interested?" "Perhaps you're interested in religion," answered his host. Newman considered for a moment. "Not actively." He spoke as though it were a railroad or a mine; and he seemed quickly to feel the apparent lack of nicety. To correct this he turned to Madame de Cintré and asked whether she was a Roman Catholic.

Satire invaded the portrait—a deep satire—but James loved Newman. Toward the end of his life he spoke of his young "infatuation" with his subject, and though by this he particularly meant an artistic absorption, his personal devotion was likewise plain. He revealed his hero as a man whom Madame de Cintré could love—

that creature "tall, slim, imposing, gentle, half *grande dame* and half an angel; a mixture of 'type' and simplicity, of the eagle and the dove." It was Newman's goodness which drew her; but this alone would not have sufficed for the daughter of an old race if goodness had not been joined with an essential dignity.

But while Madame de Cintré and Valentin perceived the genuine stature of Newman others of his family remembered their prejudices. When Madame de Bellegarde first received Newman, knowing his wish to marry her daughter, she sat small and immovable. "You're an American," she said presently. "I've seen several Americans." "There are several in Paris," said Newman gaily. "Oh, really? It was in England I saw these, or somewhere else; not in Paris. I think it must have been in the Pyrenees many years ago. I'm told your ladies are very pretty. One of these ladies was very pretty—with such a wonderful complexion. She presented me with a note of introduction from some one—I forget whom—and she sent with it a note of her own. I kept her letter a long time afterwards, it was so strangely expressed. I used to know some of the phrases by heart. But I've forgotten them now—it's so many years ago. Since then I've seen no more Americans. I think my daughter-in-law has; she's a great gadabout; she sees every one."

Even the gentle Madame de Cintré furthered the critical note, perhaps from a mild notion that Newman would be amused. "I've been telling Madame de la Rochefidèle that you're an American," she said as he came up to her in her salon. "It interests her greatly. Her favorite uncle went over with the French troops to help you in your battles in the last century, and she has always, in consequence, wanted greatly to see one of your people. But she has never succeeded until tonight. You're the first—to her knowledge —that she has ever looked upon." Madame de la Rochefidèle lifted an antique eyeglass, looked at Newman from head to foot, and at last said something to which he listened with deference but could not understand, for Madame de la Rochefidèle had an aged and cadaverous face with a falling of the lower jaw that impeded her utterance. Madame de Cintré offered an interpretation. "Madame de la Rochefidèle says she's convinced that she must have seen Americans without knowing it." Newman considered that she might have seen many things without knowing it; and the French visitor, again speaking in an inarticulate guttural, said that she wished she *had* known it. This interchange was followed by the polite approach of a very elderly gentleman who declared that almost the first person he had looked upon after coming into the world was an American, no less than the celebrated Doctor Franklin. But he too, in the circumstances, could hardly have known it.

The animus of James, who has so often been pictured as a happy expatriate, mounted as such episodes recurred. At the great reception given by the Bellegardes for Newman after the announcement of his engagement to Madame de Cintré, he was introduced to their friends by her elder brother. "If the Marquis was going about as a bear-leader," wrote James stormily, "the general impression was that the bear was a very fair imitation of humanity." James even made a comment on wordly society which might have derived from one of the early wise, wandering Yankees; its like had been heard in *Fashion*. "Every one gave Newman extreme attention: every one lighted up for him regardless, as he would have said, of expense: every one looked at him with that fraudulent intensity of good society which puts out its bountiful hand but keeps the fingers closed over the coin." Nearly fifty years later James could betray an enduring bitterness. "Great and gilded was the whole trap set, in fine, for his wary freshness and into which it would blunder upon its fate."

When the catastrophe came, when the Bellegardes broke their word and Claire was commanded to withdraw from her engagement, Newman was rejected and publicly humiliated because he was American: they found themselves unable to tolerate that circumstance in relation to their family. He was rejected on the score of manners—the old and vexing score. He should have known that to ask the old Marquise to parade through her own rooms on his arm the evening of the ball would be almost an affront. When the journey was accomplished and she said, "This is enough, sir," he might have seen the gulf widening before his eyes. His commercial connections were held against him; and James pointed the irony of the objection. The Bellegardes were shown as sordidly commercial; in shrewdness they far outdistanced Newman. He was beaten indeed because he was incapable of suspecting the treachery accumulating against him. At the end Newman was unable to maintain his purpose of revenge against the Bellegardes; he destroyed the scrap of evidence which would have proved their earlier inhuman crime. His act is not overstressed; a deep-lying harshness gave stringency to Newman's generous impulses. But the contrast is firmly kept.

With all the preordained emphasis these characters are rounded and complete. The integrity of Valentin was placed against the unscrupulous coldness of his older brother. Claire, with her lovely purity, lights the black picture created by the Marquise. If the balance seems to be tipped down by the inclusion of Mademoiselle Nioche and her deplorable father, there is always Mrs. Bread. As a great artist James had moved immeasurably beyond the simple limits of the original fable. A genuine tragedy was created whose elements were tangled deep in inalienable differences. At the last Newman was unable to understand either the character or the decision of the woman he so deeply loved. Circling across the sea and the American continent, he returned again to Paris by an irresistible compulsion, and at twilight one evening, a gray time, walked to the convent of the Carmelite order in the Rue d'Enfer and gazed at the high blank wall which surrounded it. Within, his beloved was forever enclosed, engaged in rites which he could never understand, withdrawn for reasons which he could not fathom. He could never pass beyond that wall, in body or in spirit. The image was final, and became a dramatic metaphor: in the spelling of the old fable the outcome had changed from triumph to defeat. Defeat had become at last an essential part of the national portraiture.

Oscar Cargill

From *The Novels of Henry James*

IT WAS in an "American horse-car," according to James's recollection, that the germinal idea for *The American* came to him. ". . . I found myself, of a sudden, considering with enthusiasm, as the theme of a 'story' the situation in another country and an aristocratic society, of some robust, but . . . cruelly wronged, compatriot: the point being in especial that he should suffer at the hands of persons pretending to represent the highest possible civilization. . . . He would arrive at his just vindication and he would fail of . . . vulgarly enjoying it. . . . All he would have at the end would be therefore just the moral convenience, indeed the moral necessity, of his practical, but quite unappreciated, magnanimity . . ."[1] If this is a true account, and there is no reason to

From *The Novels of Henry James* by Oscar Cargill (New York: The Macmillan Co., 1961), pp. 41-61. Copyright © 1961 by Oscar Cargill. Reprinted by permission of The Macmillan Co.
[1] *The Art of the Novel: Critical Prefaces by Henry James,* ed. Richard P. Blackmur (New York, 1934), pp. 21–22. James's recollection of the homely origin of his tale possibly led Constance Rourke to surmise a connection with one of the most popular farces of the day, Tom Taylor's *Our American Cousin* (1858), which "achieved its first great success when James was a lad of fifteen; the play created an immense volume of talk, and was con-

suppose that it is not, James consciously began *The American* with the idea that his hero's native traits should be thrown into sharp and functional contrast with those of another society; he deliberately dedicated himself to the defense of the salient virtues of his countrymen.

James amplified his initial idea, however, by suggestions from many sources, the first being Turgenev:

> . . . *The American* (1877) is based largely on Turgenev's *A Nest of Gentlefolk* (1858). The home of the Bellegardes, in *The American,* is evidently also a "nest of gentlefolk." In each novel the hero does not "belong"—Lavretski's family background, half-peasant and half-landlord, is incongruous; Newman is American middle-class. Perversely, each falls in love with the rarest bird in the nest. In each novel one of the lovers has been married. . . . In Turgenev's novel Lavretski has been unhappily married and the problem derives from Lisa's religion, which will not permit her to love a married man. In James's novel, however, it is the heroine who has been unhappily married. There the past marriage becomes only a small factor in the "conflict," which consists mainly in the opposition of the aristocratic Bellegarde family to their daughter's projected marriage to the bourgeois-democratic American. . . .
>
> Another reason for shifting the past marriage to the heroine was James's desire to locate the dramatic conflict even more centrally in her consciousness. For in both novels . . . the determining "crisis" takes place *within* the heroine. It is, in James's phrase, "the dusky, antique consciousness of sin in this tender, virginal soul" [*re* Lisa] that carries the day. In each novel the conflict is resolved by the heroine's decision to enter a convent. James was fascinated by the final scene of *A Nest of Gentlefolk,* in which the hero gains admission to the heroine's convent: "She knows of his presence, but she does not even look at him; the trembling of her downcast lids alone betrays her sense of it. 'What must they both have thought, have felt,' asks the author. . . . With an unanswered question his story characteristically closes." In *The American* James reproduced both the scene and the unanswered question at the end.[2]

---

tinued for many years." "The American," *The Question of Henry James,* ed. F. W. Dupee (New York, 1945), p. 140. I can see very little in this conjecture. *The American* ran in the *Atlantic* from June, 1876, to May, 1877. It was published in book form in the latter month in Boston; the first authorized edition appeared in England in Mar., 1879. Leon Edel and Dan H. Laurence, *A Bibliography of Henry James* (London, 1957), pp. 31–33, 307; A4a, c; D259. I quote from the first authorized edition.

[2] Daniel Lerner, "The Influence of Turgenev on Henry James," *The Slavonic and East European Review,* XX (Dec., 1941), 43–44; Cornelia Kelley, *The*

James began work on *The American* shortly after reaching Paris at the end of 1875.[3] Going constantly to the theater and devouring printed plays[4] while he was developing his novel from Turgenev's *A Nest of Gentlefolk*, Henry James must have been struck by the parallel afforded to the situation in Turgenev's novel in a device being exploited with great effectiveness by Emile Augier upon the French stage—the "intrusion-plot." As many as twenty-two of Augier's twenty-five plays, according to Professor Girdler B. Fitch, utilize this device as their principal plot mechanism:

> To state this theme in its simplest form, suspending qualifications for the moment, the basic action of a typical Augier play is this: *Into a group there comes an intruder whose presence is resisted by one or more persons and accepted by one or more, with resulting conflict, until someone's eyes are opened to the true situation, to the danger, or to a possible solution.* Different outcomes are possible, but the most frequent is the elimination of the intruder.[5]

Remembering that the group "is usually the family,"[6] one is struck instantly by the completeness with which this formula covers *The American*. The "intruder" is Christopher Newman and the

---

Early Development of Henry James (Urbana, 1930), p. 241, also cites *A Nest of Gentlefolk* as a source, but does not develop the idea. She also cites "Crawford's Consistency" as a source, but while it does have a situation like that in the novel, the relationship would appear to be the other way around.
[3] Allan Wade, *The Scenic Art* (New Brunswick, N.J., 1948), p. 42, says in December, 1875. H. J. to W. D. Howells, Feb. 3rd [1876]: "Shortly after coming to Paris, finding it a matter of prime necessity to get a novel on the stocks immediately, I wrote to F. P. Church, offering him one for the *Galaxy* to begin in March, and was sending off my first instalment of M.S. when your letter arrived." *The Selected Letters of Henry James,* ed. Leon Edel (New York, 1955), p. 65. H. J. to William, Dec. 3, [1875]: "I shall speedily begin in the *Galaxy* another novel. . . ." Ralph Barton Perry, *The Thought and Character of William James* (2 vols., Boston, 1935), I, 362.
[4] "I know the Théâtre Français by heart." H. J. to William, July 29, 1876. F. O. Matthiessen, *The James Family* (New York, 1948), p. 343.
[5] "Emile Augier and the Intrusion-Plot," *PMLA,* LXIII (Mar., 1948), 274–280. We know certainly that Henry James saw the following plays by Augier: *Post Scriptum, L'Aventurière, Paul Forestier, Lions et renards, Gendre de M. Poirier, Les Fourchambault, Le Mariage d'Olympe, Les Lionnes pauvres,* and *Maître Guérin.* Wade, pp. 7, 81, 83, 85, 89, 116–117, 198, 204.
[6] "M. Emile Augier, on his social side, is preoccupied with the sanctity of the family, as they say in France; he 'goes in,' as they say in England, for the importance of the domestic affections." Henry James, "M. Augier," *The Scenic Art,* pp. 116–117. This essay appeared under "Notes" in the *Nation* on July 27, 1878.

"group" the Bellegardes; the Marquis and Marquise resist his "intrusion," but Valentin, the young Marquise, and Mme de Cintré (she, only for a time) accept it. At the end of the conflict, Newman is eliminated as a suitor for Claire de Cintré's hand. James must have rejoiced in his seized parallel, for he had few intimate acquaintances in Paris in 1876 and almost no entrée into French domestic circles.[7] His knowledge of the Bellegardes was derived largely, it would appear, from his reading of French novels and from the presentation of French nobility on the Parisian stage. If there are elements of melodrama in the depiction of the Bellegardes, they are faithfully copied from the current drama. After all, James's Marquise had merely withheld medicine from her husband and allowed him to die, but the Marquis de Puygiron, in the most famous of all Augier's plays, to protect his family name when he discovers that his defiant daughter-in-law had been a courtesan, executes her as she stands in the doorway about to depart.[8] Many traits of the Puygirons suggest those of the hostile Bellegardes. Not only *Olympe's Marriage* but other plays have a compromising "scrap of paper" in them which falls into the hands of the intruder, as does Mrs. Bread's letter, to the embarrassment of the resistants. And most plays have duels, as has *The American*.[9]

But while James was working at *The American* there was put on at the Théâtre Français a play by Alexandre Dumas, *fils*, on February 14, 1876, entitled *L'Etrangère*, which boldly infused internationalism into the intrusion-plot. James was not only drawn to this play by the extended advance notice of it in *Figaro*, which

---

[7] ". . . The slender thread of my few personal relations hangs on, without snapping, but it doesn't grow very stout." H. J. to his father, Paris, Apr. 11, [1876]. *The Letters of Henry James,* ed. Percy Lubbock (2 vols., New York, 1920), I, 45. Mervyn Jones-Evans exaggerates James's Parisian reception in 1875–1876. "Henry James's Year in France," *Horizon,* XIV (July, 1946), 52–60.

[8] *Olympe's Marriage* in *Camille and Other Plays,* ed. Stephen S. Stanton (New York, 1957), p. 226. James says, "the modern theatre has few stronger pieces than *L'Aventurière* and *Le Mariage d'Olympe. . . .*" Wade, p. 116. In "The Siege of London," the following exchange occurs betweeen Mrs. Headway and one of her companions at a presentation of *L'Aventurière:*

"I'm rather disappointed," Mrs. Headway went on. "But I want to see what becomes of that woman."

"Dona Clorinde? Oh, I suppose they'll shoot her; they generally shoot the women, in French plays," Littlemore said.

The reference would seem to be to the Augier play in which this occurs. See *The Great Short Novels of Henry James,* ed. Philip Rahv (New York, 1944), p. 234.

[9] *Théâtre complet d'Emile Augier* (7 vols., Paris, 1895).

filled most of the issue,[10] but because of his special interest in the work of Dumas, *fils*, which had provided him, as Viola Dunbar has convincingly shown,[11] with the main features of the plot of *Roderick Hudson*. James reacted violently and at length to this play:

> . . . *L'Étrangère* strikes me as a rather desperate piece of floundering in the dramatic sea. . . . The "Foreigner" who gives its title to the piece, and who is played by that very interesting actress, Mme Sarah Bernhardt, is a daughter of our own democracy, Mrs. Clarkson by name. She explains in the second act, by a mortal harangue—the longest, by the watch, I have ever listened to—that she is the daughter of a mulatto slave girl by a Carolinian planter. As she expresses it herself, "My mother was pretty: he remarked her; I was born of the remark." Mrs. Clarkson, however, has next to nothing to do with the play, and she is the least successful figure the author has ever drawn. Why she should be an American, why she should have Negro blood, why she should be the implacable demon she is represented, why she should deliver the melodramatic and interminable *tirade* I have mentioned, why she should come in, why she should go out, why, in short, she should exist—all this is the perfection of mystery. She is like the heroine of an old-fashioned drama of the Boulevard du Crime who has strayed unwittingly into a literary work, in which she is out of time with all her companions. She is, on Dumas' part, an incredible error of taste. It must be confessed, however, that her entrance into the play has masterly effectiveness. . . .[12]

L'Etrangère is a hodgepodge of theatrical motifs of the sensational kind, yet Francisque Sarcey, the best critic of the Parisian stage of the nineteenth century, while noting its limitations, praises the very American elements Henry James most objects to:

> Such is this curious play which savors both of highly comedy and cheap melodrama, an unbelievable mixture of extravagant

---

[10] See "Paris Revisited," Wade, pp. 39–40. This was the first of James's articles to appear in the New York *Tribune*. It was published on Dec. 11, 1875, but dated "November 22nd, 1875."

[11] "A Source for *Roderick Hudson*," *Modern Language Notes*, LXIII (May, 1948), 303-310. The source is *L'Affaire Clemenceau* which James had reviewed in the *Nation* on Oct. 11, 1866. See RODERICK HUDSON, p. 21.

[12] Wade, pp. 57–58; under the heading "Parisian Affairs," this was James's ninth letter to the N.Y. *Tribune*. Published on Mar. 25, 1876, it is dated Feb. 28, 1876; hence James saw *L'Etrangère* early in its run. Of course he may have got some details from the *Figaro* account, which, however, he says was lacking in particulars.

fantasies, of strange boldnesses, of shocking vulgarities, and of incomparable passages; where two masterly scenes, that of the introduction of Mrs. Clarkson in the first act and that of the discussion with the Yankee in the fifth, stand out against a background of pure inventions which remind one of Ponson du Terrail and of d'Ennery. . . .[13]

Henry James's reaction to the play appears, from this comparison, to be the result of a jealous Americanism. "To be a cosmopolite is not, I think, an ideal," James wrote after *The American* had appeared; "the ideal should be to be a concentrated patriot."[14] It is possible that this conviction was formed in him by seeing *L'Etrangère* upon the boards. Like Lowell, who introduced him to the French theater, James could be very critical of his countrymen,[15] but let an outsider assail them and he was up in arms.[16] A surge of patriotic indignation prompted his assault on the play in his letter to the *Tribune*, but it carried him beyond this report to make his work in hand an almost retaliatory response upon the French.

For, although he scoffed at Dumas's play, James was strongly influenced by it. Mistress Clarkson, who is divorced by her husband, has formed a working arrangement with the latter, through which he conducts all their affairs in America and sees her only occasionally; Dumas's satire of the loose domestic arrangements of some Americans probably prompted James's satire of the almost casual relationship of the elderly Touchetts in *The Portrait of a*

---

[13] *Quarante ans de théâtre* (8 vols., Paris, 1901–1902), V, 300. For a summary of the play and commentary, see Henry S. Schwartz, *Alexandre Dumas, fils, Dramatist* (New York, 1927), pp. 71–74. Schwartz mentions, however, very few of the points which I enumerate in the next paragraph, to be got only from the play itself.

[14] *Portraits of Places* (London, 1883), p. 75. "Occasional Paris," in which this statement appears, was dated "1877" by James.

[15] An odd conjunction of elements, quite in line with my thought, appears in a letter to William, July 29th [1876]: ". . . My life there [Paris—he was at Etretat] makes a much more succulent figure in your letters, my mention of its thin ingredients as it comes back to me, than in my own consciousness. A good deal of Boulevard and Third-rate Americanism: few retributive relations otherwise. I know the Théâtre Français by heart!" *Letters*, I, 51.

[16] He rejoiced in the prospect of disaster coming to Dumas: "I went for an hour to Flaubert's. . . . they were talking about the great theatrical event, Alexandre Dumas's *L'Etrangère*. . . . They all detest Dumas—very properly, and predict for him a great fiasco before long." H. J. to Alice James, Feb. 22 [1876], *Parisian Sketches*, ed. Leon Edel and Ilse Lind (New York, 1957), p. 242.

Lady. Mistress Clarkson's unusual given name, "Noémie" (Mr. Clarkson has named a town for her in Utah), gave Mlle Nioche her alliterative first name in *The American.* The mistake of M. Mariceau in giving his daughter Catherine in marriage to the Duke may have suggested to James Claire de Cintré's first marriage. Because Mr. Clarkson is responsible for the return of the compromising letter to the Duchesse de Septmonts, James has his hero refrain from exhibiting to the Bellegardes' Parisian circle the character-destroying and incriminating letter which comes into his possession. Of course, Clarkson does merely a gallant thing; he is not beset, in this connection, by a torturing moral dilemma, as Newman is. James's conception of his hero, aggrandized by patriotism and constant reference to Turgenev's Lavretski, confers on him values beyond Clarkson's reach; the simple action of the latter, however, is the germ of his own.

But in the main, as I have said, the effect of *L'Etrangère* upon James was to create a desire to refute the play; in *The American* everything goes by opposites: Clarkson is restive to get back to the West to make more money in gold mining; Newman is a Californian who has made his money quietly in manufacturing and has no desire to return to business. Both Clarksons pointedly mention large sums of money in casual conversation; Newman scarcely alludes to his wealth. Mistress Clarkson pays 25,000 francs to be received by the Duchesse and to drink a cup of tea (her hostess smashes the cup afterwards); whereas Newman is indifferent to society and wishes only the hand of Claire. While Clarkson is free in gunplay—he not only defeats three robbers in the West but as a substitute duelist kills the villain of the play, the corrupt Duc Maximin de Septmonts, Newman abjures all violence and looks upon dueling as barbarous. Indeed, the whole torturing sequence which leads to Count Valentin's foolish duel and death may be thought of as an eloquent refutation to the supposition, which might have arisen from Clarkson's stage behavior, that Americans took human lives lightly and found gunplay a sport. Clarkson declines to view the Septmont picture gallery, declaring he has other things to do; James locates Newman in the Salon Carré of the Louvre in the first episode of his novel, not to demonstrate his cultivated taste in pictures, but to show that, unlike Clarkson, he had a yearning to know something about art, even if his country was not so rich in galleries as Europe. Further, there is apposite allusion to art and music throughout James's novel. Mistress

Clarkson has long been animated to revenge her mother upon all males; in his struggle Newman finally rejects the revenge motive.[17] Look upon *The American* as a reply to *L'Etrangère* and James's reasons for choice of episode and motivation, in instance after instance, become transparent. He is justifying American ways against a European caricature of them.

In reacting against Dumas's play, James not only made the intruder morally victorious, but by emphasizing all the antitheses between the play and his novel, and between Newman and the hostile Bellegardes, brought about a true clash of character based upon *mores*—and created what is really the first international novel.[18] In "A Passionate Pilgrim" (1871), "The Madonna of the Future" (1873), and "Madame de Mauves" (1874), James had been unconsciously yet instinctively moving toward the creation of the international tale,[19] yet it took precisely the combination of circumstances described here to produce the authentic thing; a catalyst like *L'Etrangère* was needed to precipitate *The American*, for the international novel is not one in which a foreign setting gives merely a romantic interest, as in the tales of F. Marion Crawford or Ernest Hemingway. An international novel is one in which a character, usually guided in his actions by the *mores* of one environment, is set down in another, where he must employ all his individual resources to meet successive situations, and where he must intelligently accommodate himself to the new *mores*, or in one way or another, be destroyed. It is the novelist's equivalent of providing a special medium in a laboratory for studying the behavior of an organism, only here it is a device for the revelation of character. James appears to have been the first to realize the potentialities of the type and to bring it to full development.[20]

---

[17] Alexandre Dumas, *fils*, *L'Etrangère: Comédie in cinq actes* (Paris, n.d. [1908], 148 pp.

[18] "*The American* (1877) was an almost scientific study of internationalism. . . ." Ernest A. Baker, *The History of the English Novel* (10 vols., London, 1938), IX, 248.

[19] James in his Preface to *The Reverberator* describes these tales as "sops *instinctively* thrown to the international Cerberus formidably posted *where I doubtless then didn't quite make him out*, yet from whose capacity to loom larger and larger with the years there must already have sprung some chilling portent." *The Art of the Novel*, p. 194. (Italics mine.)

[20] Oscar Cargill, "The First International Novel," *PMLA*, LXIV (Dec., 1958), 418–425, in which the claim made for the Baroness Tautphoeus by Howells [*Heroines of Fiction* (2 vols., New York, 1901), II, 139] is examined, along with those which might be made for Turgenev and even Howells himself, and all are seen as less valid than one which might be made for Henry James.

The author of an international novel assumes responsibilities that localized fiction does not impose. He must avoid distortion in the opposition of characters and, while generalizing on national traits, keep a sense of the uniqueness, in every instance, of the representatives of those traits. Yet the form does of itself provide a refuge for the novelist—if all can be seen from the protagonist's point of view, his obtuseness or blindness may conceal the author's limitations in reporting the milieu and behavior of the protagonist's opposition. Reflecting on *The American* some thirty years later, James remembers his "infatuation" with making Newman "consistent," with giving the effect through him to the novel of a *"centre."* "He supremely matters; all the rest matters only as he feels it, treats it, meets it." Admitting one lapse in the treatment of his protagonist when he permits Newman to neglect Mme de Cintré after he has been introduced to the Bellegarde circle as her fiancé but at the same time indicating that attention to Claire which evoked response from her must "add to her eventual shame," James is still content to let the novel "stand or fall by his more or less convincing image."[21]

James managed the externals and patent indicatives of his representative American with ease. Newman's appearance and his speech[22] avoid the caricature and burlesque of current stage presentations of the Yankee, but nevertheless suggest his limitations in dress and address. On the score of his psychology James endowed Newman with the most salient trait of his countrymen—a self-confidence and easy assurance, which is not egotism, carries him unruffled through most situations. "You've got something it worries me to have missed," said Valentin. "It's not money, it's not even brains, though evidently yours have been excellent for your purpose. It's not your superfluous stature. . . . It's a sort of air you have of being imperturbably, being irremovably and indestructibly

---

[21] *The Art of the Novel*, pp. 37–39. The fault is really deeper than the neglect which the novelist acknowledges. Though chiefly concerned with textual improvements, Isadore Traschen has brilliantly demonstrated James's lack of knowledge of passion in this novel. James is interested "in the ethical problems love created rather than in love itself." "James's Revisions of the Love Affair in *The American*," *New England Quarterly*, XXIX (Mar. 1956), 43–62.

[22] Particularly a kind of unconscious brag in his talk. See especially the speech in which he tells the Tristrams he wants "the best article in the market" for a wife. "Newman could only have been drawn by a countryman who had studied . . . his admirable and truly national characteristics," M.L.H., "Mr. Henry James, Jr., and His Critics," *The Literary World*, XIII (Jan. 14, 1882), 11.

(that's the thing) at home in the world. . . ." Newman explains his assurance by saying it's his consciousness "of honest toil, of having produced something . . . somebody has been willing to pay for," but when Valentin objects that he has known successful manufacturers of soap who have left him "perfectly cold," Newman settles for "just the regular treat of being an American citizen. . . . That sets a man right up." In Walt Whitman's perfect phrase, Christopher Newman "stands aplomb in the midst of things."

Newman's assurance is responsible for some of his lesser traits, for example, his utter candor. It contains an admixture of naïveté, when it is a handicap to him, but it is also tinged with shrewdness, and may be dry and winey. "It's a great pity you have made me your enemy," he tells Mme de Bellegarde, after complimenting her on her "pluck." "I should have been one of your greatest admirers." Another by-product of the hero's confidence is his magnanimity. Newman is consistently tolerant. Before he goes abroad, he abandons an advantage over an unscrupulous opponent, sacrificing with it sixty thousand dollars, just as he fails later to press his advantage over the Bellegardes. "Newman's revenge was to forego his revenge," writes Ernest A. Baker; "he, at any rate, could afford to be generous."[23] But this is ever so slightly the wrong emphasis; it treats his action as an advantageous tactic rather than as the product of "one of the large and easy impulses generally characteristic of his type."[24] Secure and unassailable in his manliness, if not in his manners, Newman's silent commentary on the conduct of the Bellegardes, his judgment, is the hardest thing they have to bear.

---

[23] *The History of the English Novel,* IX, 249. Messrs. R. B. West, Jr., and R. W. Stallman have an interesting suggestion in regard to Newman's destruction of the letter: "He could not use his own weapon (the letter) to fulfill the merely formal purpose of upholding his honor; although Valentin felt obliged to use his (pistols) in an affair involving a woman for whom he no longer cared. . . ." *The Art of Modern Fiction* (New York, 1949), p. 585.
[24] *The Art of the Novel,* p. 22. Note Newman's response to Valentin's surmise that they will "get on," being so very different, "like fish and fowl," as not to quarrel: " 'Oh, I never quarrel,' said Newman rather shortly." p. 122. Joseph Wood Krutch (*The Modern Temper,* New York, 1929, pp. 155–160) appears to read too much into Newman's conclusion that "revenge was not his game" when he makes it an effect of James's aestheticism—"he realized that an act of revenge was inappropriate to that style." Mme de Talyas gallantly throws her lover's letters into the flames when she sees no purpose any longer in using them to keep the lover from her rival in Octave Feuillet's *The Amours of Phillippe,* tr. Mary N. Sherwood (Philadelphia, 1860). But see Floyd C. Watkins, "Christopher Newman's Final Instinct," *Nineteenth-Century Fiction,* XII (June, 1957), 85–88, which reveals a final weakness in Newman.

Newman is so exemplary of the American type that he lacks something as an individual. It is in an effort to individualize him, probably, that Babcock, the young Unitarian minister from Dorchester, Massachusetts, is introduced into the story. Newman's easy acceptance of Europe and "want of moral reaction" readily mark him off from this dutiful seeker of "impressions," with his guidebook knowledge of pictures and churches but with his secret detestation of Europe; the points of difference between the two men, however, seem relatively inconsequential in the action of the story. We are hardly shown those personal traits of the hero which have a particular appeal for Claire de Cintré, who surely was not prepared to fall in love with just the pure American type, whatever his material possessions. As a matter of fact, the grounds for affection between Newman and Valentin are much more clearly exposed than those for deep attachment between Newman and Valentin's sister.

However satisfactory Newman may be judged to be as a type, he is ever so much less satisfactory as a *"centre."* It is true that James keeps him in focus admirably, but it is not true that he endows him with much perceptivity, despite his final illumination. Constance Rourke has cited the supreme example of his obtuseness: "He should have known that to ask the old Marquise to parade through her own rooms on his arm the evening of the ball would be almost an affront. When the journey was accomplished and she said, 'This is enough, sir,' he might have seen the gulf widening before his eyes."[25] That Newman grows cannot be controverted—but he puts a distance between himself and Tom Tristram, which is not a measure of tremendous enlargement, although it awakens admiration in Tristram's wife. If he transcends the Bellegardes—and he does—it takes a tremendous wrench to land him there. "A story in which the main actor is so uninitiated can bear no very close resemblance to the story of Isabel Archer or Lambert Strether," writes Joseph Warren Beach. "There is no revelation of anything through Newman's consciousness—nothing depends upon his *understanding*. There is in fact no spiritual dilemma. That is why the book is not among the greatest of its author's. . . ."[26] Identification with Christopher Newman on the

---

[25] Rourke, p. 151.
[26] *The Method of Henry James* (New Haven, 1918), pp. 204–205. Baker agrees with this (IX, 249), but Michael Swan, in his introduction to the Chiltern Library edition (London, 1949, p. 3), sees Newman as "an embryo Strether, the hero of *The Ambassadors*." Swan even imagines "James, had all the circumstances of his life been different, growing into a Newman." This is extravagant.

reader's part, because of his imperceptivity, presents considerable difficulty, save perhaps to a most ardent American reader.[27]

James failed to avail himself thoroughly of the most obvious advantage in making Newman imperceptive, namely, of ascribing to Newman's ignorance whatever James himself did not know about the Bourbon faction in the old aristocracy of France. Yet the Bellegardes, in the main, are permitted to reveal themselves too directly. Overestimating the consequence of Dumas's *L'Etrangère*, he replied to it in kind (for which he might be forgiven), but at some hazard to the accuracy of his portraiture. It is not to be wondered at that, unaware of his provocation, Marie-Reine Garnier has charged James with "slander." James's conception of the deportment of Valentin (who, on Newman's first visit to the Rue de l'Université, for his diversion offers to show him over the house, "like the guardian of a museum") and that of Urbain's wife (who chatters like a magpie before a stranger) is held grossly untrue to their breeding. James's representation of the aristocratic milieu is held to be nothing less than "right in the realism of the description of manners."[28] In a generally favorable study of James, Marie-Anne de Bovet challenges the verisimilitude of *The American* on the same score. It is incredible to her that Madame de Cintré should have been prevented by her mother from marrying the man she loved, and she concludes that James's Faubourg Saint-Germain is wholly legendary.[29]

It might be noted, however, that the Bovet and Garnier critiques were written, respectively, twenty-three and fifty-nine years after the time represented in the novel, and that the one farthest removed is the more severe. This raises the question if James's recent French critics are in a better position than he was to know

---

[27] Yet James returns to the defense of Newman as a *"centre"* in the Preface to *The Princess Casamassima* where he lists him as one of his "mirrors." *The Art of the Novel,* p. 70.

[28] *Henry James et la France* (Paris, 1927), pp. 35–36. See also Cyrille Arnavon, *Histoire littéraire des Etats-Unis* (Paris, 1953), p. 293. One cannot help wondering if there is not also in the French criticism of James on this score a bit of tart retaliation. He had criticized Balzac for exactly what he is now criticized for: "He [Balzac] began very early to write about countesses and duchesses; . . . the manner in which he usually portrays the denizens of the Faubourg St. Germain obliges us to believe that the place they occupy in his books is larger than they occupied in his experience." *French Poets and Novelists* (London, 1878), p. 93.

[29] "Un Ecrivain cosmopolite, Henry James," *La Nouvelle Revue* (Feb. 1, 1891), pp. 532–556. Cornelia Kelley, however, cites the obedience of French girls to their mothers that James noted in "A French Watering Place," New York *Tribune,* August 12, 1876. *The Early Development of Henry James* (Urbana, 1930), p. 241, note 15.

what the *ancien régime* was like. Cornelia Kelley expressed just such a doubt in regard to the Garnier critique and cited a more nearly contemporary French review by Thérèse Bentzon,[30] who is not surprised to find Newman "so living, so real" but is "amazed" at the fidelity of the drawing of Valentin de Bellegarde, "one of the last specimens of gallant, expansive, spiritual French gentlemen," and that of the young Marquise de Bellegarde, and especially that of Mlle Nioche. Though, as we have seen, James relied almost wholly on the current French drama for his portraits of the aristocracy and seems as faithful in his representations as those on the contemporary stage (which appears itself to have been hostile, if not limited), he perhaps had some small, special knowledge of the characters signalized by Mlle Bentzon. For Noémie Nioche, James may well have drawn upon his memory of one of his French governesses, Mlle Augustine Danse, whom he terms an "adventuress" and compares with Becky Sharpe:

> The daughter of a political proscript who had but just escaped . . . and who wrote her micawberish letters from Gallipolis, Ohio, she subsequently figured to my imagination . . . as the most brilliant and most genial of irregular characters, exhibiting the Parisian "mentality" at its highest, or perhaps rather at its deepest, and more remarkable for nothing than for the consummate little art and grace with which she had for a whole year draped herself in the mantle of our innocent air.[31]

For the young Marquise, James may have drawn on a long-remembered vision of a titled young lady whom he saw on one of his journeys, boldly supplemented by his acquaintance with the central figure in Octave Feuillet's *La petite comtesse* (1857).[32] And is it not possible that Count Valentin was created in much the same way, from a remembered person and supplementary reading?[33] Valentin indeed might have been concocted from the genial

---

[30] Not "M. Bentzon" as given by Miss Kelley, p. 241; "Bentzon" is the pseudonym of Marie Thérèse Blanc. *Revue des Deux Mondes* (May 1, 1883), pp. 126–127. See also T. Bentzon, *Les Nouveaux romanciers américains* (Paris, 1885), pp. 71–92.

[31] *A Small Boy and Others* (New York, 1913), pp. 307, 308, 328–330.

[32] *Notes of a Son and Brother* (New York, 1914), pp. 55–57.

[33] James recalls being in his youth at Homburg and Baden-Baden in those "September days in which French society, so far as it was of the Empire, at least, moved more or less upon [those places]; and we met it in expressive samples. . . ." *Notes of a Son and Brother*, p. 54. Did James recall a "sample" in Valentin? I think the impressions were very general and less than his reading.

John La Farge[34] and anyone of the numerous young counts who appear in the plays of Augier, Dumas, Marivaux, and Scribe. None of these persons is conventional or representative, and James safely risked their portraiture.

For readers partisan to Newman, his implacable opponents, Urbain and his mother, are drawn with convincing skill. Yet neither such a reader's satisfaction nor their proximity to their prototypes on the French stage is a wholly valid argument for their authenticity. In their exchanges with Newman they are perhaps more convincing than in their behavior. The Marquis is given the greatest line in the book when, in response to Newman's revelation that Valentin had apologized for his family, Urbain murmurs but two words, *"Le misérable!"* Though James presents her as without scruple, the elderly Marquise in all her encounters with the hero carries her high role successfully, allowing Newman only an instant of penetration into her fear. Adopting the rather shoddy device of making Mme de Bellegarde French only by marriage, James covered himself against minor implausibilities, but his skill in legitimizing her growing coldness toward Newman because of his unwitting gaucheries compensates for the evasive tactic.

James's greatest failure in the book is not to acquaint his reader thoroughly with his heroine; he withheld a great deal about Claire de Cintré in the mistaken notion that any development other than fragmentary of her character would detract from the presentation of his hero;[35] actually Newman's values would have been increased by a clearer definition of what he valued. Least of all did James properly prepare us for Claire's decision to seek refuge in a convent. With the example of Turgenev's Lisa before him, James should have early given us intimation of Claire's spiritual dedication, of her propensity toward asceticism, which leads her in her final scene with Newman to declare, in response to his entreaties, "I'm as cold as that flowing river!"[36] It is as though James saw her final act as

---

34 *Ibid.,* pp. 63, 84–96.
35 With this protected type of eligible young Frenchwoman James plainly had no acquaintance at all. His autobiographical volumes and letters (as far as published) confirm this.
36 The limitation of Claire de Cintré is her coldness, her perfection. Tom Tristram calls her "a great white doll of a woman who cultivates quiet haughtiness." Like Mrs. Tristram, who says of Claire, "She is perfect!" her own brother Valentin declares, "I have never seen a woman half so perfect or so complete"; but he also says, "She looks like a statue which had failed as stone, resigned itself to its grave defects, and come to life as flesh and blood, to wear white capes and long trains." Even Newman cannot tell with

wholly a check upon her family—they could no longer use her as a pawn—and as though the novelist lacked a sense of the convent as refuge and the religious life as a vocation. Newman, who had not been deeply disturbed at the prospect of marrying a Catholic —which would have been a very momentous issue with most of his Protestant contemporaries in 1868, reacts from her announcement that she will become "A nun—a Carmelite nun. . . . For life, with God's leave" with characteristic Protestant horror, not unshared, seemingly, by his creator:[37]

> The idea struck Newman as too dark and horrible for belief, and made him feel as he would have done if she had told him she was going to mutilate her beautiful face or drink some potion that would make her mad. . . .

The horror is protracted in later scenes as Newman views and visits the convent in the Rue d'Enfer; then the reflective reader recalls Newman's tolerant indifference to the perturbations of the Reverend Mr. Babcock earlier in the novel. It becomes apparent that James has substituted a general anticlericism, inadequate for his crisis, for Turgenev's careful development of Lisa's religious convictions. *The American* devotes as much attention to religion as does *A Nest of Gentlefolk*, but the emphases are wrong, and as a consequence, Claire is far beneath Lisa as a source of interest.[38]

---

her where urbanity ends and sincerity begins. Ray B. West, Jr., and R. W. Stallman (*The Art of Modern Fiction*, New York, 1949, p. 857) write, "Her name suggests a halo; Claire de Cintré—an arch of light—a lighted window, the bright window through which the reader peers towards perfection." One wonders, however, if James (sometime resident of New England) did not have the colder lunar rainbow in mind. So deeply introverted a type was beyond the powers, not only of James, but of any fictionist in the seventies to describe. Further, had James shown Claire before the end in all her complexity, he would have made his hero a more deluded man than he now appears to be. But what else could have been his sense of his heroine when he told Howells that marriage between his central pair was "impossible"? Claire occupies a position between Mme de Mauves and Mrs. Ambient.

[37] One should note, of course, a totally different attitude toward the Church in "The Altar of the Dead." I have wondered if, in Newman's reaction to the Church at this time, there is not a sly reference to the "Newman controversy." Newman became a Cardinal in 1879.

[38] ". . . with this lady, altogether, I recognize a light plank, too light a plank, is laid for the reader over a 'dark' psychological abyss. The delicate clue to her character is never definitely placed in his hand." *The Art of the Novel*, p. 39. The reader is not alone if he has failed to understand Claire. Her own brother Valentin, and obviously her family, misunderstands her. Valentin assures Newman, "But in proportion as Claire seems charming, you may fold your arms and let yourself float with the current; you are safe. She is so good!" But the reader should see beyond the Bellegardes.

If, with the important exception of Claire de Clintré, the French characters of *The American* are passably accurate in a static way, the action in which James involves them is not so persuasively plausible. "I was so possessed of my idea that Newman should be ill-used," James acknowledges, ". . . that I attached too scant an importance to its fashion of coming about." The Bellegardes "would positively have jumped" at Newman, according to James's later judgment; that they did not, gives them a "queer falsity."[39] One wonders also at Mme de Bellegarde's dark crime; though she is made utterly capable of it, as capable as Regina Giddens in *The Little Foxes* (who duplicates her act), it does not seem wholly plausible that she could not have accomplished her purpose of marrying Claire to M. de Cintré without the death of her husband. In the New York edition of the novel Claire speaks of the "curse" upon her house, and James adds a phrase to the deathbed note of M. de Bellegarde, explaining the reasons for his wife's action: "It's in order to marry my beloved daughter to M. de Cintré *and then go on herself all the same.*" Royall Gettmann thinks that this is a hint that Mme de Bellegarde herself was carrying on an adulterous affair with M. de Cintré and intended to continue it after her daughter's marriage.[40] This idea is fully developed in the stage

---

39 *Ibid.*, p. 35. Pelham Edgar, *Henry James: Man and Author* (London, 1927), p. 243, gives another example of too facile plotting: ". . . the first difficulty was evidently to establish relations for Newman in the great world. To this end the out-at-the-elbows device of a convent friendship had to be adopted. . . . Claire de Cintré refused to let her childish intimacy with the present Mrs. Tristram die. . . ."

40 "Henry James's Revision of *The American*," *American Literature*, XVI (Jan., 1945), 292. Mr. Gettmann remarks that this adds "a stronger motive for the murder." It also makes *The American* more like the plays James was seeing on the Parisian stage, with their inevitable adultery. John A. Claire (in *"The American:* A Reinterpretation," *PMLA*, LXXIV [Dec., 1959], 613–618) suggests "that Mrs. Bread, the true mother of Claire de Cintre, was a blackmailer claiming both Newman and the Marquise de Bellegarde as victims; that Newman, by dint of his characteristic American naïveté and his opacity as a judge of character, was completely 'taken in' by her ruse; and that Claire's refusal to accept Newman in marriage came as a direct result of her having been informed by the Bellegardes of her true parents—the old Marquis and his 'meanest of mistresses,' Catherine Bread." I am not prepared to accept this suggestion, for (1) it would too closely duplicate the forcing device used with Christina in *Roderick Hudson,* (2) it would ennoble Mme de Bellegarde beyond any intention James would have appeared to have at this time, (3) with Newman's intention to take Claire to America, it would make strange their opposition to the marriage, (4) it calls for giving credence to the Marquise's invention that Catherine Bread had been her husband's mistress, and (5) the idea of Mrs. Bread's blackmailing the Marquise is untenable on the basis of their characters.

version of *The American;*[41] hence the interesting question arises: Did James restore an original feature of the crime or add an implication after dramatization had revealed the weakness of Mme de Bellegarde's motivation? We know that a difference of opinion developed between Howells, the editor of the *Atlantic* in which *The American* was serialized, and Henry James over the ending of the novel, but the only surviving letter would seem to indicate that Howells had protested merely because the ending was "unhappy," for James points out that Claire and Newman would have made "an impossible couple."[42] Perhaps, as a concession to Howells, James toned down the Marquise's crime, but I do not incline much to that view.

Even with the original serial ending, James's invention rarely led him so far astray as in this novel, and his later defense of it as a romance validated by the convincing quality of its hero[43] only underlines its limitations. "By the time *The American* was written," Pelham Edgar ventures, "he had already achieved his emancipation from romantic extravagance. Christopher Newman has no impulse to scale the walls of the Convent of the Rue d'Enfer, but paces the streets like an ordinary disappointed man."[44] The extravagances of the plot, in all deference to Mr. Edgar, conflict with the substantial realism of the materials of the story and produce a disharmony that is limiting in its effect. In correcting Dumas, James fell into the ways of the sensational dramatist, with the result that *The American* is a weaker novel than *Roderick Hudson,*[45] which preceded it, and *The Portrait of a Lady,* which

---

41 Robert P. Falk, "Henry James and the 'Age of Innocence,'" *Nineteenth-Century Fiction,* VII (Dec., 1952), 184–185.

42 *The Selected Letters of Henry James,* ed. Leon Edel (New York, 1955), pp. 68–69: "I quite understand that as an editor you should go in for 'cheerful endings'; but I am sorry that as a private reader you are not struck with the inevitability of the *American* dénouement. I fancied that most folks would feel that Mme. de Cintré *couldn't,* when the finish came, marry Mr. N[ewman]; . . . they would have been an impossible couple. . . ."

43 "I had been plotting arch romance without knowing it. . . ." *The Art of the Novel,* p. 25. But note also (Preface to *The Golden Bowl*): ". . . the many sorry businesses of *The American*" (p. 344). This does not indicate that the complacency of the earlier Preface was lasting.

44 Edgar, p. 242. Contrast: "La fin du récit est rempli d'invraisemblances, non pas dans les sentiments, mais dans les situations; on l'attribuerait volontiers à Miss Braddon, aux romanciers à sensation, plutôt qu'à un raffiné tel que Henry James." Bentzon, *Les Nouveaux romanciers américains,* p. 82.

45 Henry Popkin shrewdly observes that *The American* "is a particular favorite of those readers who do not generally care for James." "The Two Theatres of Henry James," *New England Quarterly,* XXIV (Mar., 1951),

came after. A portion of that weakness may be assigned to the fact
that it was a pioneer experiment with the international novel and
the further fact that James wrote as an emotionally aroused American.[46]

---

70. "In spite of the morbid plot and the final futility of the principal character as well as of the book itself, Mr. James in many ways is very nearly at
his best in *The American.*" John Curtis Underwood, *Literature and Insur-
gency* (New York, 1915), p. 76. William Lyon Phelps calls it "a work of
genius . . . this masterpiece . . . this great work of art." *The Advance of
the English Novel* (New York, 1919), pp. 315–316. "Christopher Newman
remains for all time the wistful American business man who spends his life
hankering after the fine things he has missed." Van Wyck Brooks, *The
Pilgrimage of Henry James* (New York, 1925), p. 102. A notable exception,
however, occurs to me: John Macy, who described Henry James as "like a
great scientific mind imprisoned with a few bugs," attacks *The American*
for lack of realism: "If Mr. Newman . . . had been an Englishman, the story
would have gone just as well. . . . What Newman says is not distinctly
American in substance, in tone, in turn of phrase." *The Spirit of American
Literature* (New York, 1911), pp. 328–330.

[46] There are two good articles on the revisions which James made in *The
American* for the New York edition. Isadore Traschen devotes his paper
largely to the way in which James emphasized and elaborated on certain
aspects of Newman's "innocence" and "barbarism," which are one and the
same. "An American in Paris," *American Literature,* XXVI (Mar., 1954),
67–77. Max F. Schulz, in a more elaborate essay, extends the treatment of
Newman, showing how the added details are frequently to aspects most
offensive to the Bellegardes, while their characters are made more intolerant,
passionate, and intemperate. Metaphors involving castles and wines are
extended throughout the text. Newman's operations are inflated: instead of
making soap, he now makes "mountains of soap," and a five-figure income
becomes a six-figure one. "The Bellegardes' Feud with Christopher Newman:
A Study of H. J.'s Revision of *The American,*" *American Literature,*
XXVII (Mar., 1955), 42–55. James's chief problem in revision, I would
suggest, was to make a novel, which was essentially a reply to a satire that
had been completely missed in America, completely plausible just as fiction.
It was an almost insuperable task.

"Americans in Europe are *outsiders;* that is the great point thrown into
relief by all zealous efforts to controvert it. . . . We are not only out of the
European circle politically and geographically; we are out of it socially,
and for excellent reasons. We are the only great people of the civilized
world that is a pure democracy, and we are the only great people that is
exclusively commercial." Henry James, "Americans Abroad," *The Nation,*
XXVII (Oct. 3, 1878), 208–209. The whole article, pertinent to Newman,
was brought to my attention by Dan Laurence.

4. Special Approcahes

George Knox

Romance and Fable in James's
The American

Throughout the latter half of the nineteenth century, American novelists and critics disputed the conflicting merits of the Novel *vs.* the Romance. This controversy also involved the popular campaign to call forth a (or the) Great American Novel, and the question whether this anticipated prose substitute for the Great American Epic would be realistic or fabulous. In any case, it had all kinds of imperatives imposed upon it. The great work, when it appeared, should manifest the evolution of American cultural identity and the growth of American intellectual and moral consciousness. Howells wryly teased these formulators. James wisely ignored the clamor and expressed amusement at their portentous expectations. He molded and adapted the novel as independently as Hawthorne and Melville, his American predecessors in the Romance. Rejecting pat local colorist and realist criteria, James also refused to be hustled into thematic *cul-de-sacs*. When *The American* was published, it underwent critical scrutiny as a candi-

From *Anglia,* LXXXIII (1965), 308–322. Copyright © 1965 by Max Niemeyer Verlag. Reprinted by permission of publisher and author.

date for the Great American Novel, but by critical consensus did not qualify. The novels of Howells and James which dealt with European scenes were anathema to the purist prophets of nationalism in fiction.

James was from the start a Romancer, inclined to go below the surfaces of life to psychic depths, and above to levels of ideals and principles. His narratives and details are built solidly on fable bases. In some ways we may be better prepared to realize his intentions than his contemporaries. The nineteenth-century critic, even a shrewd professional like Howells, was not so well equipped as the twentieth-century exegete. There is no complete critic of course, and the terminologies and perspectives of any era reveal many factors while preventing one from seeing others. Today, the study of folklore, myth, ritual drama, psychoanalysis, archetypal imagery, and other matters has provided us with views which are often valid in discussing novels written before our time. Perhaps one can talk about James's Romances without violating them if one applies some more recent notions of form and structure. It is already literary history that the great Romances of "the later phase" have intriguingly opened up under the probings of critics sensitive to fairy-tale motifs, religious legendry, and symbolic patterns. (One critic, for example, has rather ingeniously revealed James's indebtedness to Swedenborgianism, in image and theme[1]). Although James himself has not told us everything he was doing, this does not prove that certain bodies of lore and knowledge are not in his work and that particular terms long in use since his day do not accurately describe them.

Regardless of the prescriptions of nineteenth-century editorial propagandists, James made his own challenges and without any blaring of horns proceeded from the seventies onward to write his Romances mostly on the European scene, about Americans in Continental settings. Even Howells, the prophet and practitioner of realism *par excellence*, had finished his writing career before the

---

[1] Quentin Anderson, *The American Henry James* (New Brunswick, New Jersey, 1957). See also Anderson's "Henry James, His Symbolism and His Critics," *Scrutiny,* XV (1947), 12-18. Leon Edel's "Architecture of Henry James's New York Edition," *New England Quarterly,* XXIV (1951), 169-178, is excellent on patterns, figures, secrecy, "mystification." R. L. Gale has written on art and Freudian imagery, Royall A. Gettman on James's revisions in *The American,* J. Patterson on the language of adventure. One finds at least a dozen long articles on James's use of metaphor and symbol. Names associated with cluster, ritual, archetypal, and myth criticism are: Caroline Spurgeon, Maud Bodkin, Kenneth Burke, Francis Fergusson, and Northrop Frye.

triumph of native realism occurred. It is also significant that during the most productive years of Howells and James, critics repeatedly spoke of reducing American life to fable outlines in order more effectively to express character types and traits common to all sectors of the society. The American Romance, it was often said, should reflect that most remarkable paradox of American life—the mixture of the fabulous-ideal and the realistic-banal (the "commonplace"), which Howells first defined and justified as the province of fiction. Critics asked that novelists treat photographically the surface of life and at the same time mirror out of the depths of "national consciousness" what might be called today racial images, archetypal patterns, and cultural fables.

Both Howells and James, good friends but far apart in their art, theorized about this matter of "typical embodiments," and it is with this as a starting point I have chosen to discuss *The American*. I wish to talk about it not as an unsuccessful try at the Great American Novel, but merely as a Romance, which James in his retrospective Preface almost tediously explained it to be[2]). In the 1870's the fuss about the realistic Novel and the fabled Romance reached new heights of enthusiasm; *The American* was published in 1877. James chose to delineate the "invasion" of a thirty-six-year-old self-made millionaire, a kind of benign robber-baron, looking for art and an aristocratic ("first-class", as he put it) wife. Later, James confessed that at that time he had not known such a person at close range, nor had he any real acquaintance with the Faubourg St. Germain. Perhaps partly because of this alleged ignorance, he resorted to the typifying mode. But I think his later apologetic remarks were made partly in response to critics who pointed out the lack of "verisimilitude" in characterization. His first intent had been to write a cultural parable, *i.e.*, a Romance.

The name of his hero (and James even refers to him in the novel as "our hero"), Christopher Newman, is an obvious clue to some degree of allegorical intention[3]). Furthermore, I think it is clear

---

[2] Preface written for the New York Edition, 1907, Copyright 1907 by Charles Scribner's Sons; reprinted in *The Art of the Novel*, ed. R. P. Blackmur (New York, 1947). All quotations are from the 1877 edition. I have avoided giving text references for most quotations as being distractive.
[3] First, I think we notice that as a kind of reverse Christopher Columbus, Christopher Newman (new man) is coming to Europe on a voyage of discovery. Second, and fainter as a clue, he may share, parodically, something of the legendry that has grown up around St. Christopher, patron saint of ferry boatmen and travellers. St. Christopher transported people across water; Newman would have taken Claire across the Atlantic to America.

that James worked with myth patterns from beginning to end. During the heavy tourism in James's day, many travellers had returned home feeling somewhat inadequate culturally. And, in spite of all the shouting about cultural independence, the clamor about a Great American Novel, or Romance, was unmistakably colored by feelings of inferiority. James, in writing *The American*, knew these feelings at first hand. Significantly, Ezra Pound has thought of James as the Europeanized American artist *par excellence* and refers to him in Canto VII: "And the great domed head, *con gli occhi onesti e tardi* / Moves before me, phantom with weighted motion, / *Gravi incessu*, drinking the tone of things, / And the old voice lifts itself / weaving an endless sentence."

Since its publication, the novel's critics have placed too literal an emphasis on the purely social factors instead of reaching into its psychic depths for the fable. Indeed, one does not have to reach deeply. The fable is from one angle the story of the American innocent ("passionate pilgrim").[4] The equations he worked out in *The American* reappear with fine variations in novel after novel; they are like the image clusters of a poem).[5] James's Romances have been widely discussed in the terminology of poetry criticism, dramatic alignments being thought of as analogous to the symbolic patterns in poems. Therefore, we will discover that Newman's tale projects a cultural fable of success and failure, superimposed on various fairy-tale motifs, allusions to marriage-immurement themes in Renaissance paintings, and the employment of eighteenth-century Gothic conventions[6]). In developing his conventions, and stock plot, he ties the narrative together by interconnecting two climacteric incidents: the Carriage Crisis in Chapter II and the Church Crisis in Chapter XXVI. All minor incidents clustering around these moments reflect and support them. The fairy-tale

---

[4] Newman is after a wife, mainly; but his culture-seeking counterpart is a young Unitarian minister, native of Dorchester, Mass., "in spiritual charge of a small congregation in another suburb of the New England metropolis." Benjamin Babcock is his name. His digestion is weak, "and he lived chiefly on Graham bread and hominy" in Europe. He is passionately serious about "art."

[5] James's revisions of *The American* heighten the aristocratic qualities of the French nobility and accentuate the rustic qualities of Newman. The major aspect of the revision is the multiplication of images which cluster around the protagonist and his adversaries.

[6] Many of James's novels derive from the Gothic tradition. The short novel which comes quickly to mind is *The Turn of the Screw*. A recent critical work on the Gothic is Leslie Fiedler's *Love and Death in the American Novel* (New York, 1960).

elements converge in Newman's failure to release and then ᴗ possess the princess, or sleeping beauty, and constitute the reversal that results from the hero's cultural inferiority[7]), in spite of all his insistence to Valentin that he is a "civilized" man. At least he knows what he wants: "Goodness, beauty, intelligence, a fine education, personal elegance—everything, in a word, that makes a splendid woman." Claire has these things, plus noble birth, and thus is Newman's "dream realized."

But though the Bellegardes succeed in thwarting him at the moment when success seemed sure, the Yankee is not to be cheated. He triumphs morally through renunciation. This told American readers what they wanted to know—that it is they (and their "hero") and not the European aristocrats who are really superior. Therefore, the "mythology" or fable falls between a nineteenth-century realist mode of innocents-abroad critical fiction (cf. De Forest, Mark Twain, and William Dean Howells) and the idealizations of Romance[8]). The structure is a cyclic analogizing of states of ignorance-innocence and wisdom-wickedness. In addition to a play on the Dantean upward climb of the hero, we find shadows of the nineteenth-century "proletarian" (Algeresque) striver, as in *Roderick Hudson* (1876), *The Rise of Silas Lapham* (1885), *The Princess Casamassima* (1886), *The Damnation of Theron Ware* (1896). Each of these in its way exemplifies the Romance mode. Twain's *A Connecticut Yankee in King Arthur's Court* (1898) pushed the Romance genre to the outer limits of parody, becoming also one of the major (and darker) anti-utopian fictions in American literature.

Christopher Newman emerges ironically from blithe cultural ignorance into sad experiential awareness at moments of moral decision or during climacteric adventure, neatly foreshadowed and carried through the stages of perilous journey, crucial struggle, and exaltation of the hero. Two major "clusters" are involved: 1. Newman's encompasses images of spring, summer, dawn, vigor, fertility and passionate love. 2. The Bellegardes' comprises images of darkness, winter, sterility, old age, and death. James was indeed right in his Preface, stating that he had written "archromance" without

[7] Claire, at one point reads a fairy story entitled *Florabella and the Land of the Pink Sky*. She is obviously identified with "poor Florabella" but I cannot find this story or its prototype. James may have concocted it.
[8] The really impressive predecessor of *The American* in the ironic-Romance mode is Hawthorne's *The Blithedale Romance* (1852). The novel is a mine of mythic and ritual motifs.

entirely realizing it at the time. Newman looks upon the Bellegardes as the Frenchmen of "tradition and Romance"; conversely,
like the Duchess, they tend to see him, in terms of American
folklore, as combining the characteristics of a western giant in
seven-league boots, Benjamin Franklin, and a "Duke of California"
who will someday become President of all the Americans. In his
Preface James admits that the outlines of the story took shape in
"the deep well of unconscious cerebration" and hints at psychological abysses in characterization.

However, Newman's journey toward realization of his "dream",
the Odyssey which will earn him his name, is a journey toward
reality. His quest is marked by the two aforementioned "somersaults," as he calls them. In Chapter II, he tells Tristram how he
had planned revenge on a business associate who had played him
"a very mean trick." He had taken a hack for Wall Street and
fallen into a "sleep or reverie." Awakening, he felt "mortal disgust"
for the thing he was going to do. " 'It came upon me like that!'—
and he snapped his fingers—'as abruptly as an old wound that
begins to ache.' " Indeed, this is an important moment. The hack
looked to him "as if it had been used for a great many Irish
funerals" (and like a "hearse"), and Newman expostulates: "this
immortal, this historical hack." The language in the following
passage must be examined carefully for connotations of a change
of heart—we may even say "conversion." This term denotes the
importation of significances from a religious context, but Newman's
change is sudden and fundamental. I do not think it necessary to
discuss whether James *intended* the connotations which I discover
in the following passage:

> We pulled up in front of the place I was going to in Wall Street;
> but I sat still in the carriage, and at last the driver scrambled down
> off his seat to see whether his carriage had not turned into a
> hearse . . . I told the man to drive down to the Brooklyn ferry and
> to cross over. When we were over, I told him to drive me out into
> the country. As I had told him to drive for dear life down town, I
> suppose he thought me insane, perhaps I was, but in that case I am
> insane still. I spent the morning looking at the first green leaves
> on Long Island. I was sick of business; I wanted to throw it all up
> and break off short; I had money enough, or if I hadn't I ought to
> have. I seemed to feel a new man inside my old skin, and I longed
> for a new world. When you want a thing so very badly you had
> better treat yourself to it. I didn't understand the matter, not in
> the least; but I gave the old horse the bridle and let him find his

way. As soon as I could get out of the game I sailed for Europe.
(Ch. II)

Not only do we detect a particularly American hubris, but
unmistakable connotations of this psychic event impel us to secu-
larize a term again and call it "rebirth." Moreover, three stages
of the quest to follow are anticipated (the *agon*, or conflict; the
pathos, or death struggle; and the *anagnorisis*, or discovery). These
classical Greek dramatic terms need not be restricted to theater, for
they name an archetypal situation. Geographically, the passage is
filled with nineteenth-century ironies. Newman, who had made his
fortune out West, now plans a voyage to the Old World to realize
its worth.

In addition to the prefiguration of several "wall" encounters, or
barriers where Newman experiences bafflement and exclusion, a
series of "somersaults" (conversions) are hinted at. But Newman
is not only acted upon; he also affects changes around him. Valentin, taken in by Newman's "prose version of the legend of El
Dorado", consents to make a new life for himself, under Newman's
sponsorship, in America. He is willing to accept "an 'opening' in an
American mercantile house": "I make myself over to you. Dip me
into the pot and turn me into gold." Other stock quest motifs are
adumbrated; the romance hero sometimes fulfills a messianic function. He is the deliverer from an upper world, in this case the
American do-gooder in his nineteenth-century avatar. Newman is
distantly (in the future) related to Mark Twain's Yankee Hank
Morgan ("Sir Boss"), who sets out to Americanize "medieval"
England and ends up blowing it to pieces.

Other motifs and images extend into ironic conceits—eye and
water imagery, for example. From *The Odyssey* to *Portrait of the
Artist as a Young Man*, the crossing over bodies of water implies
moving from known to unknown, from familiar to mysterious,
from innocence to experience, from New World to Old. Even the
repeated allusions to Claire's eyes seem to merge into the overall
pattern. Mrs. Tristram describes Claire's eyes as "clear and still."
But she adds: "She is cold, calm and hopeless." Four months after
meeting Claire, Newman remembers her eyes: "If he wanted to
see more of the world, should he find it in Madame de Cintré's
eyes? He would certainly find something there, call it this world or
the next." Newman constantly ponders her "mystery" in terms of
black and white, of still and flowing water. Whereas convent life is
"peace and safety" to Claire, Newman tends to think about her

joining the Carmelites in terms of the pit, in Gothic imagery of "moonshine and bloodshed."

Claire connotes brightness and light, as when Newman first sees her dressed in dazzling white, wearing a blue cloak, diamonds glittering in her hair. She is, after all, the princess. But Cintré also connotes an arch in a Romanesque church, which is dark. The last time he sees her, she is dressed in black and shows a "monastic rigidity" as she walks across the "dark oaken floor, polished like a mirror". Newman thus shuttles from shadow into light, from winter into spring. In Chapter XIX, he suffers through the death of his brother-in-law-to-be when Valentin dies of duelling wounds in Switzerland.

Newman wanders from the death scene into an Alpine spring.

> The day was brilliant; early spring was in the air and in the sunshine, and the winter's damp was trickling out of the cottage eaves. It was birth and brightness for all nature, even for chirping chickens and waddling goslings, and it was to be death and burial for poor, foolish, generous, delightful Bellegarde. Newman walked as far as the village church, and went into the small grave-yard beside it, where he sat down and looked at the awkward tablets which were planted around. They were all sordid and hideous, and Newman could feel nothing but the hardness and coldness of death.[9]

Later on, Mrs. Bread says that Claire is a fair peach,

> with just one little speck. She had one little sad spot. You pushed her into the sunshine, sir, and it almost disappeared. Then they pulled her back into the shade and in a moment it began to spread. Before we knew it she was gone.

In Chapter XX, after Valentin's death, Newman receives the letter from Claire, asking that he come to see her. He goes

> straight to Paris and to Poitiers. The journey takes him far southward, through green Touraine and across the far-shining Loire, into a country where the early spring deepened about him as he went.

---

[9] At this time M. Ledoux, the physician, "a youthful and rather jaunty practitioner," gives Newman (who relieves his bedside watch) a small volume "which the surgeon recommended as a help to wakefulness, and which turned out to be an old copy of *Faublas*. This is James's short title of Louvet de Couvray's *Les Amours de Chevalier de Faublas* (1789–90), which offers some ironic parallels to Newman's love-quest.

This ironically recalls his crossing over by ferry to the green spring on Long Island, to his trip of recovery "out in the country." He drives to the village of Fleurières and passes, en route, through a Perilous Cemetery onward to the vicinity of the Bellegarde château, his Perilous Castle. He sees Madame de Bellegarde on the arm of the dark Urbain, and in the background the pall-bearers and mourners. A few days later he visits the ancient pile and is awed and depressed by its Gothic antiquity, "a horrible rubbish-heap of iniquity to fumble in!" James's description of the château, with its two-arched bridge, moat, dull brick walls, ugly cupolas, deep-set windows, pinnacles of mossy slate—all mirroring themselves in the river—suggests ominous enchantment.

The ominous element lies beneath a tranquil surface of water, a metonymic reminder of Claire and her ambiguous depths of mystery—or of French culture itself.[10] Such play on surface and depth, radiance and morbid darkness, reminds us of James's humor in contriving the name of her English suitor, Lord Deepmere, the shallow nobleman who also fails to win the princess. The Bellegarde name is an obvious pun suggesting that "urbane" Urbain and his mother will guard Claire, *la belle*, who stands for the beauty which Newman would "buy"; *i.e.*, they must beautifully guard her. Or, considering the word Cintré—*ceintrée*—one might say, "Elle est fort bien ceintrée!" Tristram ironically describes Claire to Newman, before their meeting, "as plain as a pike-staff."

After James has unfolded all the melancholy decay, Newman is ready to penetrate the barrier, "the vast iron gate, rusty and closed." Gaining entrance, he meets Claire in black.

> He was dismayed at the change in her appearance. Pale, heavy-browed; almost haggard, with a sort of monastic rigidity in her dress, she had little but her pure features in common with the woman whose radiant good grace he had hitherto admired. She let her eyes rest on his own, and she let him take her hand; but her eyes looked like two rainy autumn moons, and her touch was portentously lifeless.

Several pages later, Newman challenges her to defy her family and marry him; he accuses her of mocking him. "I am cold", answers

---

[10] Edith Wharton's *The Custom of the Country* offers many ironic cultural parallels, but Newman's role is split between Undine Spragg and Elmer Moffatt. Since Wharton's viewpoint is sympathetic with the French aristocracy, she makes Elmer a ruthless exploiter and Undine an American sprite without a soul. The novel is filled with watery imagery, used to caricature cultural immersion, and crossings. Cf. her "The Great American Novel", *The Yale Review*, XVI (1927), 646–656.

Madame de Cintré. "I am as cold as that flowing river." This
exemplifies the life-death paradoxes, as in the green village land-
scape, when Newman comes upon the cemetery unexpectedly: "the
very headstones themselves seemed to sleep, as they slanted into
the grass . . ." The river which encircles the château is strangely
"green." And, when Newman comes out of Valentin's death room,
and looks at the "awkward tablets which were *planted* around,"
we realize how life and death, surface and depth, winter and summer have become confused in this new-old world.

Madame de Cintré exclaims that she cannot disobey, judge, or
criticize her mother: "*I* can't change!" Newman counters bitterly,
and echoes the somersault motif of earlier speeches: "I must
change—if I break in two in the effort!" It is shortly after this
exchange that Claire tells him she is going into a convent, "for life,
with God's leave." After she expands upon this theme, Newman
conjures an image of her muffled in "ascetic rags," and entombed
in a cell,

> a confounding combination of the inexorable and the grotesque.
> As the image deepened before him the grotesque seemed to expand
> and to overspread it; it was a reduction to the absurd of the trial
> to which he was subjected.

But in spite of all his beseeching she replies that it is inevitable
and nothing he can do will prevent it.

> This time he took her hand, took it in both his own. 'Forever?' he
> said. Her lips made an inaudible movement and his own uttered
> a deep imprecation. She closed her eyes, as if with the pain of
> hearing it; then he drew her towards him and clasped her to his
> breast. He kissed her white face; for an instant she resisted and for
> a moment she submitted; then, with force, she disengaged herself
> and hurried away over the long shining floor. The next moment
> the door closed behind her.

So far, "our hero" has made his initial symbolic crossings: undergone a premonitory and preparatory rebirth; sailed on the passionate pilgrim's voyage; suffered the trials among the hostile,
alien tribe; experienced vicariously both physical death (Valentin's)
and spiritual death (Claire's "entombment"); wandered through
graveyards; crossed the moat into the Perilous Castle; and endured
a final rejection. Repulsed by France, he travels to England where
he remains until midsummer before sailing "the summer seas" to

New York. Then he crosses the continent to San Francisco, half of his exile-and-return pattern, having gone through "the vague circle which sometimes accompanies the partly-filled disk of the moon." Toward the end of winter, he returns to Paris, visiting the Rue d'Enfer, where Claire had already taken the veil of the Carmelites on her twenty-seventh birthday, and assumed the name of her patroness, St. Veronica, who wiped the face of Christ with her veil.

"Sister Veronica has a lifetime before her", wrote Mrs. Tristram to Newman. This incites him to visit the convent. The affair had not yet taken on the lineaments of reality for him. Before he had returned to America the whole matter had been turned over and over in his mind.

> If such superb white flowers as that could bloom in Catholic soil, the soil was not insalubrious. But it was one thing to be a Catholic, and another to turn nun—on your hands! There was something lugubriously comical in the way Newman's thoroughly contemporaneous optimism was confronted with this dusky old-world expedient. To see a woman made for him and for motherhood to his children juggled away in this tragic travesty—it was a thing to rub one's eyes over, a nightmare, an illusion, a hoax.

On his return he visits the convent, trying to peer in. But no light comes through its crevices, only darkness visible.

When the sounds of the service reach him, Newman angrily feels something grim and triumphant directed toward him, something in the "genuflections and gyrations" in "the mouthing and droning" that signified triumph over him. He listens for Madame de Cintré's voice, and in the very heart of the tuneless harmony he imagines he makes it out. He feels a great emotional surge at the sound of this "impersonal wail," and unable to bear it any longer he arose and made his way out, tears in his eyes. James tells us, however, that his emotions are based on illusion, inasmuch as Claire had obviously "not yet had time to become a member of the invisible sisterhood." He makes his last visit to the Rue d'Enfer on a day which "had the softness of early spring; but the weather was gray and humid." James ingeniously merges deathly and verdant connotations when he describes that dumb, deaf, inanimate place.

Thus the quest, combining both comic and tragic conflicts and tones, leads to a vision of the "law," a revelation of that which is and must be, a closing of doors. "Comically," the resolution will discard the motive of *lex talionis*, or revenge by the hero who has provoked enmity through the purity of his motives. It is an American irony that the hero's original act of presumption provokes the unjust rejection and the inhumane imprisonment of the princess. An antithetical or counterbalancing movement must be set up when the innocent hero plots revenge. Comically, again, the movement will not be completed. Another epiphany, a moral revelation, causes a reversal and an abnegation. The hero first disturbs the balance of society and then must restore it. The wish fulfillment dream completes itself as a peculiarly American archetype. The victory must be moral transcendence.

On his final visit he turns away from the walls behind which the princess is bewitched, "lost beyond recall," directing his steps in horror and disgust ("the charm utterly departed") toward Notre Dame! We encounter in the passage which follows the crucial crossing and revelation. He turns away with heavy heart,

> . . . but with a heart lighter than the one he had brought. Everything was over, and he too at last could rest. He walked down through narrow, winding streets to the edge of the Seine again, and there he saw, close above him, the soft, vast towers of Notre Dame. He crossed one of the bridges and stood a moment in the empty place before the great cathedral; then he went in beneath the grossly-imaged portals. He wandered some distance up the nave and sat down in the splendid dimness. He sat a long time; he heard faraway bells chiming off, at long intervals, to the rest of the world. He was very tired; this was the best place he could be in. He said no prayers; he had no prayers to say. He had nothing to be thankful for, and he had nothing to ask; nothing to ask, because now he must take care of himself. But a great cathedral offers a various hospitality, and Newman sat in his place, because while he was there he was out of this world. The most unpleasant thing that had ever happened to him had reached its formal conclusion, as it were; he could close the book and put it away. He leaned his head for a long time on the chair in front of him; when he took it up he felt that he was himself again. Somewhere in his mind, a tight knot seemed to have loosened. He thought of the Bellegardes; he had almost forgotten them. He remembered them as people he had meant to do something to. He gave a groan as he remembered what he had meant to do; he was annoyed at having meant to do it; the bottom, suddenly, had fallen out of his revenge. Whether it was Christian charity or unregenerate good nature—what it was, in the background of his soul—I don't pretend to say . . . (Ch. XXVI)

As in the initial passage, Newman makes a crossing after a crisis. He is again exhausted, experiencing a quiescence, a spiritual *stasis*, or *accidie*. Most significantly, his trial has reached its *formal* conclusion and he can "close the book"—signs that James is filling out a fable structure, the formula of a prototypical romance quest.

Literally, Newman has merely crossed a Seine bridge and entered Notre Dame, as countless American tourists have done without symbolic significance, but this is a fable, a fairy tale, and figuratively and ritually he has come from Hell (Rue d'Enfer—"the charm utterly departed"), the "spell" lifted. He is en route to Redemption (the Church), a parodic kind to be sure, but we cannot miss the implication that his visit to Notre Dame ends his ironic harrowings-of-hell, for, instead of releasing the soul of Claire from bondage, he releases his own. The final confrontation of the "pale, dead, discolored wall" behind which the enchanted princess is irrevocably immured, "seemed the goal of his journey: it was what he had come for. It was a strange satisfaction and yet was a satisfaction; the barren stillness of the place seemed to be his own release from ineffectual longing." At this point we see the parallel with the Carmelite nuns who wail "their dirge over their buried affections and over the vanity of earthly desires." Released from "ineffectual longing," he could enter the church and emerge graced for the final trial in his quest.

Thus, the transformation incident in New York has prefigured a cycle of trials en route to spiritual realization, with crucial losses and frustrations for the hero, and for us inversions of conventional sentimental and romantic expectations. The loss of his egoistic, naive, vengeful, and innocent selfhood, dramatized in a seasonal ritual of metamorphosis, results in an unexpected kind of victory, a gain in moral strength. In other words, our hero earns his hitherto adventitious name. In fact, "living death" is the metaphoric key to existence which Newman must finally understand.

> His wound began to ache with its first fierceness, and during his long bleak journey the thought of Madame de Cintré's 'life-time', passed within prison walls on whose outer side he might stand, kept him perpetual company. Now he would fix himself in Paris forever; he would extort a sort of happiness from the knowledge that if she was not there, at least the stony sepulchre that held her was.

After his "illumination" at Notre Dame, he goes to his rooms, kept by Mrs. Bread, asking her to pack the portmanteau she had just unpacked the evening before. Mrs. Bread's comments are an undersong, or choric accompaniment to Newman's thoughts.

" 'Dear me, sir,' she exclaimed, 'I thought you said that you were going to stay forever,' " upon which Newman explains: " 'I meant that I was going to stay away forever.' " This answer ironically echoes the "happy forever after" line of the fairy tale before the authorial voice intrudes: "And since his departure from Paris on the following day he has certainly not returned. The gilded apartments I have so often spoken of stand ready to receive him; but they serve only as a spacious residence for Mrs. Bread, who wanders eternally from room to room, adjusting the tassels of the curtains, and keeps her wages, which are regularly brought her by a banker's clerk, in a great pink Sèvres vase on the drawing-room mantleshelf." The gilded sepulchre will not receive him physically again, of course, but it has already in essence (spiritually) received his old self.

Newman's return to Paris completes the final arc of the circle. At least he is ready to go to Tristram's and throw the damping document into the flames, the remnant of his old impure self, "like a page torn out of a Romance." Pitifully, the Bellegardes were for him the ideal Frenchmen of tradition and Romance. Romance becomes reality when lived and suffered through; just as the Bellegardes rejected Newman "in the abstract" and gave him up for an "idea," so Newman had to lose his "ideal" in the trials of a quest and make a moral renunciation. Glory and wisdom and beauty are not to be cheaply and easily purchased, as Newman had bought bad copies made by Mademoiselle Noémie Nioche. Newman's innocent eyes must see anew; he must reach his formal conclusion. His eye "was full of contradictory suggestions, and though it was by no means the glowing orb of a hero of romance," it contained "almost anything you looked for." He began his stay in Europe feeling "as simple as a little child, and a little child might take me by the hand and lead me about."

He began not knowing the difference between surface and depths, art and reality (as hinted in the running play on Claire's eyes). Justice is done. He gets his reality. As his sometime travelling companion and fellow innocent, the Unitarian minister Mr. Benjamin Babcock, wrote to him about "the immense seriousness of Art" and of the impossibility of their being *en rapport* as pilgrims to the shrines of beauty: "I hope you will continue your travels; only *do* remember that Life and Art *are* extremely serious." In Chapter XXVI, where the second illumination occurs, Newman confesses his sense of "being a good fellow wronged," a sign of incompleteness in his redemption, perhaps of a constitutional flaw in the American character. He reflects "with sober placidity that at least there were no monuments of his 'meanness' scattered about the world." But James makes us think of poor Claire in the Rue d'Enfer and of the pink Sèvres vase on the mantleshelf in the empty gilded apartments, and of Mrs. Bread's "wages" accumulating therein—apt tokens (in a reverse sense) of what Reverend Sewell in Howell's *The Rise of Silas Lapham* (written a few years later) would call "realistically" the "economy of pain".

John A. Clair

The American: A Reinterpretation

APART FROM the fact that Henry James may not have wished to create such a black and white situation—the innocent American lamb thrown to the continental wolves of Paris—in his novel *The American* it is possible that the author himself may have expected a less simple interpretation of his novel than that which such scholars and critics as Joseph W. Beach, Constance Rourke, and even F. O. Mathiessen have afforded it. To accept the popular interpretation of the work as a rather transparent story of the victimization of a "good natured" American by a Borgia-like Parisian family seems to involve an oversight of much explicit and implicit information in the novel, which suggests that Mrs. Bread, the true mother of Claire de Cintre, was a blackmailer claiming both Newman and the Marquise de Bellegarde as victims; that Newman, by dint of his characteristic American naïveté and his opacity as a judge of character, was completely "taken in" by her ruse; and that Claire's refusal to accept Newman in marriage came as a direct result of her having been informed by the Bellegardes

From *PMLA,* LXXIV (December, 1959), 613–618. Copyright 1959 by the Modern Language Association of America. Reprinted by permission.

of her true parents—the old Marquis and his "meanest of mistresses," Catherine Bread. This deeper significance which underlies the surface action and characterizations in the novel is indicated by James in the Preface to the 1907 edition of *The American* when, speaking of the novelist as painter, he states:

> It is a question, no doubt, on the painter's part, very much more of perceived effect, effect *after* the fact, than of conscious design—though indeed I have ever failed to see how a coherent picture of anything is producible save by a complex of the fine measurements. The cause of the deflexion, in one pronounced sense or the other, must lie deep, however; so that for the most part we recognize the character of our interest only after the particular magic, as I say, has thoroughly operated—and then in truth but if we be a bit critically minded, if we find our pleasure, that is, in these intimate appreciations (for which, as I am well aware, ninety-nine readers in a hundred have no use whatever. . . .)[1]

It is these "intimate appreciations" expected by the author to which he surely refers when, speaking of Claire and Newman in the Preface, he states: "The delicate clue to her conduct is never definitely placed in his hand: I must have liked verily to think it *was* delicate and to flatter myself it was to be felt with fingertips rather than heavily tugged at" (NY, xxii). If we may assume that James deliberately placed "clues" in the novel—to be found by one reader out of a hundred—might we not also assume that he employed this subtle technique to point out a deeper relationship between Mrs. Bread and the Bellegarde family? It is this relationship—Mrs. Bread as the natural mother of Claire de Cintre who has been reared by the Bellegardes (step-guardians)—which perhaps will become more clear after an examination of pertinent evidence.

Led by the author's remarks in the Preface that "Nothing . . . is in truth 'offered'—everything is evaded," and that "the delicate clue to her [Claire's] conduct is never definitely placed in his [Newman's] hand," a deeper probing of the motivations of characters, supported by several associative references in the novel, may afford a greater insight into the meaning of James's story. The author's descriptions of Claire de Cintre, except where they reflect the idealistic views of Newman, greatly resemble Mrs. Bread

---

[1] *The Novels and Tales of Henry James,* 11 vols. (New York: Scribner's, 1907), xiv-xv—hereafter referred to as NY and cited within the text.

—not the Marquise de Bellegarde. After it is established in the opening chapters that Newman cannot distinguish between the "real" and the "copy," indeed cannot distinguish between a beautiful or a plain woman, we are given repeated indications of his obtuse judgment. When Newman inquires of Mrs. Tristram if Claire is a "beauty," the cleverly evasive matchmaker replies, "She is not a very great beauty, but she's very, very beautiful; two quite different things" (NY, p. 54). Her husband, however, a frank, unromantic American living in Paris, tells Newman that Claire is "plain as a copy in a copy-book—all round o's and uprights a little slanting." The significance of Tristram's unbiased view of the heroine is only heightened when we consider his use of the words "copy in a copy-book" which recalls Newman's painful victimization by the Nioches with the "painting" copies and indicates by a clever analogy that Claire herself is a poor "copy." Newman's first sight of Claire is set down by the author: "Through the slight preoccupation it produced he had a sense of a longish fair face and the look of a pair of eyes that were both intense and mild" (NY, p. 57). But this first impression is quickly transformed by Newman into a model of physical perfection. Later in the novel the young Marquise de Bellegarde, Urbain's wife, describes Claire: "poor dear Claire didn't belong to the most pleasing type of woman. She was too long, too lean, too flat, too stiff, too cold; her mouth was too wide and her nose too narrow. She hadn't such a thing as a dimple, or even a pretty curve—or call it an obtuse angle—anywhere" (NY, p. 485 ff.). These descriptions of Claire afford us a rather composite picture of the heroine—a composite which certainly resembles Mrs. Bread, who was "tall and straight and dressed in black. . . . She had a pale, decent, depressed-looking face and a clear, dull English eye. She looked at Newman a moment, both intently and timidly, and then she dropped a short, straight English curtsy" (NY, p. 251). Mrs. Bread's stature, tall and straight, as well as the plain, long face and clear, dull eye, certainly indicates her maternal relationship to Claire. The heroine's mannerisms closely resemble the half-deferential, half "mildly audacious" attitudes of Mrs. Bread; nowhere in the novel is she pictured as having the haughty imperiousness of the Marquise, her "mother." Both the Marquis and Marquise de Bellegarde are short in stature and possess facial features radically different from those of Claire.

But James's attempt to conceal the "silver thread" of his story —Claire as the illegitimate daughter of Mrs. Bread—from those who would not have earned it is perhaps most strikingly illustrated by his deletion of certain lines from the 1907 edition of the novel. In the earlier edition, as the story nears the crucial situation, the young Marquise de Bellegarde, speaking to Newman, exclaims, "Malheureux! . . . Green bows would break your marriage—your children would be illegitimate."[2] James, however, omits the reference to illegitimate children in the later edition: "Malheureux! . . . I hope you're not going to pretend to dress your wife. Claire's an angel, yes, but her bows, already are—well, quite of another world!" (NY, pp. 309–310). Several passages in the latter scenes become quite clear when considered in the light that Claire is the natural daughter of Mrs. Bread. Urbain's remark to Newman that "I think my mother will tell you that she'd rather her daughter should become Soeur Catherine than Mrs. Christopher Newman" seems innocent enough on the surface, but a close examination reveals that nowhere in the novel to this point has Claire disclosed the name she will take as a religious; indeed, when she does take a name it is "Sœur Veronique." When we find, a short time later, that Mrs. Bread is referred to for the first time as "Catherine Bread," we can draw only two inferences: either that James erred, or that in the momentary lapse of Urbain, he intentionally placed an associative reference indicating a significant relationship to exist between Claire and Mrs. Bread. In view of the fact that James was so meticulous in his revision of the work, the latter alternative seems likely. In a similar instance in the novel, Urbain's wife refers to Claire as a "furious Anglaise" shortly before Mrs. Bread refers to herself as an "honorable Anglaise." James's technique for establishing relationships between characters is not new to scholars. In a recent article, "Religion Imagery in Henry James's Fiction," Robert L. Gale perceptively notes: "by repetition of a simple saint image concerning little Miss Osmond, James subtly underlines her real parentage. In the first volume of *The Portrait of a Lady*, " 'Ah,' cried Gilbert Osmond beautifully, 'She's a little saint of heaven!' " (NY, III, 383). A volume later, the girl's unacknowledged mother, Madame Merle, praises her in the same words—"She's a little saint of heaven" (p. 377). Isabel is the auditor of both speeches, but between them she has been enlightened as to Pansy's real mother; undoubtedly the echo falls on attentive ears."[3] It is significant that James employs the same technique in *The Ameri-*

---

[2] Henry James, *The American* (New York: Rinehart 1953), p. 205.
[3] *Modern Fiction Studies,* III (Spring 1957), 69.

can to delineate an identical relationship between Claire de Cintre and Mrs. Bread.

The characterization of "poor Catherine Bread" is central to a complete understanding of the novel, for it is solely her testimony —and Newman's belief in her testimony—which is the basis for the consideration of the Marquise and Urbain de Bellegarde as the "villains" of the story. Doubtless there are readers who have been horrified to see the Victorian stereotype of the plain-faced, old, English commonwoman of countless contrived novels toddling through the pages of Henry James; and, what is worse, to see her draw a faded letter from her bosom to hasten the denouement. Whether or not the author could be guilty of such brazen pot-boil- ing, even at the beginning of his novel-writing career, we shall let his detractors decide. In the eyes of Newman, and according to her own view, Mrs. Bread is a wronged woman living in fear for the well-being of her "child and treasure," Claire de Cintre. Her first surreptitious meeting with Newman is shown to result in the extraction of a promise from him that she will be taken along with the couple after they are married. She admonishes Newman to hasten the marriage; then, as someone approaches, leaves the room swiftly to avoid detection. Her second meeting with the hero takes place as she stands on a stairway beside "an indifferent statue of an eighteenth-century nymph, simpering with studied elegance" (NY, p. 273). After a few prying remarks by the "nymph," New- man reiterates his promise: "You know you are coming with us." Then Mrs. Bread, after mouthing a few well-timed maledictions against the Marquise, hastens away. Our next view of her is during the engagement "fete" when, at the end of the evening, she hurries up to Claire and Newman with a shawl: "Newman paused an in- stant before the old woman and she glanced up at him with a silent greeting. 'Oh yes,' he said, 'you must come and live with us. 'Well then, sir, if you will . . . you've not seen the last of me!'" (NY, pp. 332–333). By this time Newman is entirely taken by this "friendly" old woman, who evidently is intent upon gaining her security at his expense. No more is seen of Mrs. Bread until the scene in which Newman "extracts" information from her about the old Marquis' death. Early in this interrogation scene Mrs. Bread quickly becomes reticent when Newman's questions venture too near the real reason for Claire's refusal to marry:

"She knew something bad about her mother."
"No, sir, she knew nothing." And Mrs. Bread held her head very

stiff and kept her watch on the glimmering windows of the residence.

"She guessed something then, or suspected it."

"She was afraid to know," said Mrs. Bread.

"But *you* know, at any rate."

She slowly turned her vague eyes on him, squeezing her hands together in her lap. "You're not quite faithful, sir. I thought it was to tell me about the Count you asked me to come." (NY, p. 439)

Mrs. Bread then deftly turns the troublesome subject of Claire's parentage to talk of Valentin. Admittedly, the ambiguity of these lines allows a broad interpretation, but may it not also be considered as another of those "fine measurements" by which the author paints his literary picture? Certainly Mrs. Bread's plan to establish her security at Newman's expense would not be advanced by his discovery of the truth. During this revelatory scene, some obvious inconsistencies creep into Mrs. Bread's story, including her failure to explain why she did not produce the letter testifying to the murder of the old Marquis by his wife in time to save Claire from her first marriage to M. de Cintre. In the scene Mrs. Bread denies having been the Marquis' mistress, but in a later passage the Marquise affirms to Newman that Catherine Bread was "the meanest" of her husband's mistresses—an affirmation so obviously detrimental to the Bellegarde "family honor" that it may well indicate the honesty of the Marquise, an honesty which is not called into question except by Mrs. Bread and Newman.

The clearest evidence that Mrs. Bread is a blackmailer, however, is found in her description of the deathbed scene during which the old Marquis, allegedly, writes the letter accusing his wife of his murder:

He asked me to hold him up in bed while he wrote himself, and I said he could never, never trace a line. But he seemed to have a kind of terror that gave him strength. I found a pencil in the room and a piece of paper and a book, and I put the paper on the book and the pencil into his hand, and I moved the candle near him. . . . I sat on the bed and put my arm round him and held him up . . . . It was a wonder how he wrote, but he did write, in a big scratching hand; he almost covered one side of the paper. . . . I hid the paper in my dress; I didn't look at what was written on it, though I can read very well, sir, if I haven't a hand for the pen. I sat down near the bed, but it was nearly half an hour before my lady and the Count came in. (NY, pp. 453 ff.)

This description makes it impossible for us to believe that Mrs. Bread is telling the truth. It is apparent from her detailed description of the letter-writing that she certainly was able to see in which language the letter was written; indeed, she asserts that she could "read very well." Yet when Newman demands to know the contents of the letter, she replies: "I can't tell you, sir, I couldn't read it. It was French." Such an obvious contradiction can be explained either by believing that James erred in the writing of the scene, or that he deliberately draws Mrs. Bread as a scheming woman intent upon blackmailing the Bellegardes through Newman —or Newman himself, if necessary—to effect a financially secure existence for life. Since the Bellegarde fortune wanes, and Newman's marriage to Claire has been called off, her security lies in ingratiating herself to the hero. Mrs. Bread's strangely contradictory statement concerning the letter is further complicated by the fact that Newman, quite in character, fails to challenge her about the half-hour interval he is required to wait while she brings the accusatory letter to him; moreover, after a promise by Newman to tell her the contents of the letter—written, as it was, in French—Mrs. Bread shows not the slightest interest nor asks again about the information even though she and Newman converse at length in the following chapters. The question of whether or not the letter is a forgery, however, is less important than is the fact that it does contain *some* information which, if brought to light, would bring the Bellegarde family into disrepute. Indeed, the letter is not revealed as a forgery in the novel, but when Newman confronts the Marquise and her son with the written accusation, they shrug their shoulders at the "murder" charge. Upon closer examination of the letter, however, the Bellegardes find information which leads them to believe the letter to be "characteristic" of the old Marquis. The information which they feel may cause some of the dead man's "particular friends" a "real grief" is undoubtedly the allusion to his sanity carried in the cryptic line in the letter, "I am not insane." Certainly a man on his deathbed would not proclaim his sanity so vehemently if, on one hand, there were no question of his rationality or, on the other, if the charge were not true; thus the question of whether or not the letter is a forgery is less important than the implication that the Marquis was insane, and that the charge of murder was merely the product of the ravings of a lunatic, or the fabrication of a scheming mistress, or both.

A close examination of Mrs. Bread's description of the death scene shows James to have made further implications: Why was Mrs. Bread holding the old Marquis in her arms—or even present at his deathbed—if her employment was merely as the Marquise's "lady" as she states? Moreover, why is she consistently referred to as "Mrs." when it is obvious that she has been with the family since she was "too young" to hold the Marquis Urbain when he was born and there is no mention of her marriage after that time? Finally, it is significant that the author, in the revised edition of the novel, modified Mrs. Bread's characterization in several important aspects: he makes her appear more skillfully capable of deceit by improving her diction and grammar throughout the book; he places such expressions as "bete," "femme de chambre," and "Anglaise" in her vocabulary, as well as having her ask of Newman: "The Rue D'Enfer. That's a terrible name; I suppose you know what it means?" (NY, p. 251). This demonstration of a knowledge of French expressions is *not* evident in the earlier edition and may indicate that the author took greater care in the later edition to delineate more closely a characterization so important to the warp of the novel; also, perhaps, he wished to strengthen the implication that Catherine Bread was lying about her inability to read the Marquis' deathbed letter. It is obvious that Mrs. Bread, throughout the novel, follows a consistent plan.

Since, as James tells us, "the interest of everything" rests upon Newman's "interpretation" of facts, incident, and character presented to him in the novel, the characterization of Christopher Newman must be closely attended: it is through this "center of revelation" that the action of the novel is advanced. His shameful handling at the hands of the Nioches in the opening chapters shows Newman to be drawn as a gull who "often admired the copy much more than the original" (NY, p. 2); his folly in this early episode echoes like the chant of a Greek chorus throughout the story. Newman is drawn as painfully naive, egotistically possessive, and uncomfortably self-righteous; we must admit, however, with James, that he is almost offensively "good natured." After his ignominious but unprofitable experience at the hands of M. Nioche and his enterprising daughter, Noemie, Newman is similarly taken in by the romantic machinations of the artful *ficelle*, Mrs. Tristram, who challenges him to "rescue" the fair princess, Claire, from her wicked parents. At her instigation the hero quixotically rises to the occasion and sets out in pursuit of his "ideal" wife. It is noteworthy

that Mrs. Tristram later repudiates her earlier slander of the
Bellegardes, but, characteristically, Newman ignores her reversal of
attitude. Not a single time in his series of dealings with the Bellegarde family is his first reaction *not* concerned with the "success"
of his venture; it must be admitted, however, that his second
thoughts are of Claire. But his egocentric refusal to see her as
anything but an ideal companion for his "doll's house" is precisely
the "flaw" which obfuscates the real import of any situation to
which he is exposed in the story. Revelation, therefore, which comes
to us through Newman must necessarily reflect his limitations and
prejudices. For example, Claire is described by Newman as a model
of perfection, but the reader would certainly be misled were he to
overlook some inconsistencies of character which explicit information in the novel makes fact: Claire de Cintre is a strangely reticent
woman who invites Newman to call on her on the basis of a three-
minute introduction; who emerges periodically from the confes-
sionals of St. Sulpice, red-eyed and crying; who confesses to
disquieting emotions and experiences frequent outbursts of temper;
and who is deeply affected by the ravages of an early, unhappy
marriage to an elderly man. Indeed, James confesses in the Preface
to the story that he feels he had laid "too light a plank . . . over a
dark, psychological abyss" in his treatment of the heroine. Obviously if we judge Claire from Newman's point of view, we err; and
if we accept Newman's opinion of the Bellegardes as infamously
malevolent, we can also be mistaken. Although Newman loves and
trusts Valentin de Bellegarde, he has absolutely no understanding
of his young friend and chooses to ignore the fact that the Count,
certainly the most upright and honest figure in the novel, consistently holds his family's honesty and integrity to be irreproach-
able. Since Newman's judgment of Mrs. Tristram, as well as of
Noemie and M. Nioche, is completely erroneous, there seems to be
little reason to believe that he was any more perspicacious concerning the Bellegardes whom he hated, and Mrs. Bread whom he
patronized. It is Newman's incorrigible lack of insight and his
impetuous judgments which keep him ignorant of the real situation
even in his dealings with his "beloved" Claire.

In the scene in which the hero first learns that Claire has refused
to marry him, he pointedly asks her why she "obeys" the Bellegardes:

> Madame de Cintre looked across at the old Marquise measuring
> her from head to foot. Then she spoke again with simplicity.

"I'm afraid of my mother."
Madame de Bellegarde rose with a certain quickness. "This is a most indecent scene!" (NY, p. 367)

With the Marquise's excited remark the question is quickly dropped. The interchange, however, is certainly meaningful if we assume that the marriage had been called off (much as it was "called off" in *Roderick Hudson*) because the Bellegardes, knowing of Newman's naive idealization of the marriage, told Claire the truth about her parentage beforehand in order to avoid future embarrassment for both Claire and Newman, as well as for themselves. Furthermore, it is not improbable that Mrs. Bread had intimidated the Bellegardes, who saw a possible threat to Claire's future happiness in Newman's insistence upon taking Mrs. Bread "along" with them. The Marquise's reaction in the foregoing scene is explainable as an attempt to conceal that which she may have felt was a too-obvious clue to Newman of Claire's real mother, Catherine Bread.

In a later scene at Fleurieres, after Newman's impassioned pleas for Claire to recant, the following dialogue ensues:

"What right have I to be happy when—when—?" Again she broke down.
"When what?" she pressed.
"When others have so suffered."
"What others?" he demanded. "What have you to do with any others but me? Besides, you said just now that you wanted happiness and that you should find it by obeying your mother. You strangely contradict yourself." (NY, p. 412)

This passage certainly cannot be explained by the popular interpretation of the novel. Which "others" could the sufferers be if not the Bellegardes? And what else but the circumstances surrounding her birth could be meant by Claire's further statement: "about my mother it doesn't matter what you suspect and what you know. When once my mind has been made up as it is now, I shouldn't discuss these things. Discussing anything now is very vain and only a fresh torment. We must try and live each as we can. I believe you'll be happy again; even, sometimes, when you think of *me*. When you do so, think this—that it was not easy and I did the best I could. I've things to reckon with that you don't know" (NY, p. 414). After this explanation—which Newman fails to comprehend—Claire makes a further attempt to explain to him that his idealization of her left her no "loophole for escape—no chance to be the common weak creature" that she was. Once it had become clear to the Bellegardes—and to Claire herself—that Newman's intention was to "buy" an aristocratic wife, the absence of true affection on his part made it impossible for them to continue the concealment.

Finally a word must be said in defense of the Bellegardes themselves whose explicit actions in the novel show them to have dealt fairly with Newman even to the fine distinction they later seem to draw between "persuasion" and "authority" in refusing to allow Claire to marry. It must be remembered that the Bellegardes gave only their consent that Claire might be courted; because Newman, quite unasked, flaunted his wealth in their faces at their first meeting, it cannot be construed that the Bellegardes descended to a "financial arrangement." Newman's sudden proposal of marriage forced the Marquise to hold a "fete," but they had not committed themselves to a decision. It must be admitted that the Bellegardes' treatment of Newman was somewhat stiff and formal, but this is not looked upon as unfair except by Newman himself. That some greater motivation than the American's "commercialism" or the Parisian family's unexplainable malevolence was responsible for their abrupt change in attitude toward his marriage is certainly indicated. James, in the Preface to the novel, states: "The great house of Bellegarde . . . would . . . have comported itself in a manner as different as possible from the manner to which my narrative commits it." From this rather ambiguous statement, Royal A. Gettman, in his article, "Henry James's Revision of *The American*," believes that "the Bellegardes would have squeezed him [Newman] for every dollar," and also that "the murder of the old Marquis was insufficiently accounted for."[4] It would appear, however, that Gettman's view of the Bellegardes is not necessarily warranted by James's remark that the family would have "comported" itself differently: it is equally possible that the author meant that they might have revealed their position to Newman; refused his courtship of Claire at the outset; or simply acted less officiously. No appreciable changes in the characterization of the Marquise or Urbain de Bellegarde in the 1907 edition seem to indicate that James felt the characters to have needed no further support despite their lack of verisimilitude. Gettman's view that the murder of the old Marquis lacked credibility may be explained

---

4 *American Literature*, XVI (Jan. 1945), 291.

by the fact, pointed out earlier, that the basis for believing that a killing actually occurred is the less than trustworthy testimony of Mrs. Bread and the belief in that testimony by Newman. This fact then, taken into consideration with the author's remarks in the Preface and his inclusions in the text itself, make it possible to say that Newman is "saved" in a very real sense by the Bellegardes and Claire, and victimized by his "friend," Mrs. Bread. Claire de Cintre, the tragic heroine, refuses to marry Newman because of her illegitimate birth, and conceals herself from the world in the Carmelite cloister.

5. Special Achievements

James W. Gargano

Foreshadowing in *The American*

Henry James' use of foreshadowing in *The American* is sometimes so obvious as to seem labored. For example, important later events in the novel are unsubtly forecast in Newman's clairvoyant suspicion, after his first meeting with the Bellegardes, that the marquise " 'had murdered some one—all from a sense of duty, of course' " and that her son " 'at least turned his back and looked the other way while someone else was committing murder.' "[1]

One example of foreshadowing, however, the opera-scene in chapter 19, is so disguised as to have escaped critical notice. In this scene James forecasts the heroine's final retreat to a convent and sets the stage for the forsaken hero's bitter suffering. It is interesting to speculate whether James, a close student of Flaubert, may have been directed to his fictional exploitation of an opera by Flaubert's clever use of *Lucie de Lammermoor* in *Madame Bovary*.

James first associates Madame de Cintré with the convent early in the novel, when Newman, going to look at her house, finds it

From *Modern Language Notes*, LXXIV (December, 1959), 600-601. Copyright © 1959 by The Johns Hopkins Press. Reprinted by permission.
[1] *The American* (Rinehart edition), pp. 165–166.

withdrawn and "all in the shade"; "it answered to Newman's conception of a "convent."[2] Later on, at the performance of *Don Giovanni*, Madame de Cintré's future is ironically suggested in Newman's comparison of his fiancée to Donna Elvira, who, at the end of the opera, declares that she will enter a convent.[3] Though Newman insists that Donna Elvira reminds him of Madame de Cintré "in the music she sings" rather than in "her circumstances," the comparison can hardly be a fortuitous piece of chit-chat during an *entr'acte*. James artfully directs the reader's attention to Donna Elvira's fate by having the culturally naive American confess, much to the marquis' amusement, that he is curious to see how the opera will end.

The short conversation between Newman and the marquis is, indeed, remarkably full of Jamesian irony and foreshadowing. First of all, the self-confident American, unaware that the Bellegardes have decided to force Madame de Cintré to reject him, is impervious to the marquis' ironic statement that, unlike Donna Elvira, Madame de Cintré will not be forsaken. A further irony is added to the scene when the marquis jokingly compares himself to the commander, the agent of retributive justice in the opera. Since the commander is an animate statue, like the rigid, unemotional marquis, the analogy has a superficial appropriateness. That the marquis, however, should be bringing about justice, is an absurdity, for unlike the commander, who is murdered by Don Giovanni, the marquis has helped to commit a murder. Any "justice" executed by him will therefore be a travesty, a sin against honor in the interest of the unmoral social code by which he lives.

The final instance of ironic foreshadowing is contained in the indirect comparison between the faithful Newman and the dissolute Don Giovanni, about whose fate in the opera the ingenuous American inquires. When Newman is informed that Giovanni is carried off to hell, the fact seems to have little relevance to him. Yet, after Madame de Cintré decides to become a Carmelite nun, Newman, in a scene reminiscent of his first visit to her house, goes to see the convent building. In a mood which his friend Mrs. Tristram calls "wicked," he walks to the convent in the Rue d'Enfer, the Street of Hell. Filled with vengeful plans against the Bellegardes when he enters his private hell, he is softened by the utter desolation, "the barren stillness," that he beholds. Leaving this scene of

---

[2] Ibid., p. 41.
[3] Ibid., pp. 221–222.

"gratuitous dreariness"[4] with the realization that Madame de Cintré is irrecoverably lost, he finds relief in the cathedral of Notre Dame, where he surrenders all thoughts of punitive actions against his enemies. Like Don Giovanni he has descended to hell, but fortunately he returns purged; in the spirit of Christian charity, he feels "ashamed of having wanted to hurt" the Bellegardes and goes off to destroy the evidence that would at least embarrass them and might possibly ruin them.

---

[4] Ibid., p. 356.

D. W. Jefferson

[Mrs. Tristram and a "Sense of Type"]

Of the middle-aged American women Mrs Tristram, in *The American* (1877), to whom Newman owes the crucial introduction to Claire de Cintré, is of particular interest. . . . In his acute study of Mrs Tristram he depicts the restless, unsatisfied American woman. Hers is an extreme case: her husband is not a hardworking business man, but an idle expatriate. With her plain face she has lost the man she was in love with, and for perverse reasons has married a fool. Even for an American woman, she is peculiarly concerned with her own development and aspirations, which life has given her peculiarly little opportunity to further. The portentousness of outlook engendered in her by her particular conjunction of character and circumstances finds definition in an idiom saturated in Americanism:

. . . Her taste on many points differed from that of her husband; and though she made frequent concessions to the dull small fact

From *Henry James and the Modern Reader* by D. W. Jefferson (New York: St. Martin's Press, 1964), pp. 89–90. Copyright 1964 by D. W. Jefferson. Reprinted by permission.

that he had married her it must be confessed that her reserves were not always muffled in pink gauze. They were founded upon the vague project of her some day affirming herself in her totality; to which end she was in advance getting herself together, building herself high, inquiring, in short, into her dimensions.[1]

. . . Restless, discontented, visionary, without personal ambitions, but with a certain avidity of imagination, she was interesting from this sense she gave of her looking for her ideals by a lamp of strange and fitful flame. She was full—both for good and for ill— of beginnings that came to nothing; but she had nevertheless, morally, a spark of the sacred fire.[2]

James knew how to make a character-type work for him towards the building up of a novel, and a talkative, middle-aged woman with time on her hands is a valuable resource in the early part of this book. Mrs Tristram serves to draw Newman out, just as Maria Gostrey later draws Strether out. The long conversation in Chapter Three is sustained mainly by her persistent curiosity and freedom of comment. She tells him that he is "deep," threatens to say ("with a certain air") that he is "as cold as a fish," promises herself that some day she will see him "in a magnificent rage."[3] By various tactical strokes she leads him on to speak of what he really wants in life, and this brings us to the main action of the novel. Mrs Tristram is a mixed character: genuinely intelligent and kind, but with no settled sphere for the exercise of her virtues, obliged to take her mental exercise where she can, and liable . . . to amuse herself in slightly inhuman ways. After the conclusion of the Bellegarde affair, which she has helped to promote, she tells Newman that it would not have "really done" ' and musingly adds: "I should have been curious to see; it would have been very strange."[4] And she admits that curiosity was partly the motive for her participation, upon which she receives from Newman the one angry look he was ever to give her. Curiosity about how other people's lives will shape, on the part of those who are reduced to the role of spectator, is one of the common themes in James.

---

[1] *The American* [=*Amer.*], pp. 31-2.
[2] *Amer.*, pp. 33-4.
[3] *Amer.*, pp. 38-9.
[4] *Amer.*, pp. 449.

Floyd C. Watkins

Christopher Newman's Final Instinct

Henry James first conceived of *The American*, he tells us in the preface to the revised edition, in terms of a theme revolving around the character "of some robust but insidiously beguiled and betrayed, some cruelly wronged, compatriot." The character, James continued, would be wronged by "persons pretending to represent the highest possible civilization"; but at the moment of crisis, "stricken, smarting, sore, he would arrive at his just vindication and then would fail of all triumphantly and all vulgarly enjoying it."

Around this idea James developed a plot which years later he was to consider "consistently, consummately . . . romantic." In the original and revised versions it is a novel with many of the trappings of Gothic romance. Christopher Newman, the hero, becomes engaged to a young French aristocrat; the family deceitfully refuses to allow her to marry the American; and he discovers

From *Nineteenth-Century Fiction*, XII (June, 1957), 85–88. Copyright © 1957 by The Regents of the University of California. Reprinted by permission of The Regents.

a note which indicates that the obnoxious mother and brother of the heroine have committed a terrible murder. James planned for Newman to "hold his revenge," and without showing the evidence to anyone Newman does burn the note written by the dying victim. He thus obeys, as James had planned for him to do, "one of the large and easy impulses *generally* characteristic of his type." Without forgiving, he has rejected the revenge to be gained by revealing the note to the friends of the Bellegardes; "and one's last view of him," James wrote in his preface, "would be that of a strong man indifferent to his strength and too wrapped in fine, too wrapped above all in *other* and intenser, reflexions for the assertion of his 'rights.' "

The last chapter does develop the idea of Newman's goodness and his renunciation of revenge. Just before the final interview with his friend Mrs. Tristram, he reaches the decision "that of course he would let the Bellegardes go." Many a less generous person in his situation would be anxious to scale the walls of the nunnery to which his lover had retired and then to thrust the note under her nose in the hope that she would at last recognize her family's evil and renounce her nun's vows in favor of those of marriage. But during the conversation with Mrs. Tristram Newman burns the note describing the murder. This is not, however, his last action. "One's last view" of Christopher Newman in the original version, the very last view, may not be at all like the beneficent character which James had at first conceived and which he had consistently developed throughout the novel until the final one-sentence paragraph. In the last sentence, after the note is burned, "Newman instinctively turned to see if the little paper was in fact consumed; but there was nothing left of it."

This sentence has several possible interpretations. Mrs. Tristram has just told Newman that the Bellegardes trusted his "remarkable good nature" not to reveal their crime and ignominy. Perhaps Newman turns to the fire for a last glance at the burned symbol of the severe moral struggle which he has undergone. Again, he may turn to see that all the evidence is really destroyed. But he did turn "instinctively," and this adverb seems to imply that his final action is not so generous and unavenging after all. Mrs. Tristram's remark has provoked even the good Newman's lower and baser instincts, and James perhaps intended to imply that he once again has reached a moment in his moral struggle when he temporarily wishes to gain revenge. Mrs. Tristram's compliment, therefore, and her statement that "they were right" in trusting his good nature makes Newman "instinctively" wish to prove them wrong. It is of course not inconsistent with Newman's goodness for him to undergo such a struggle and indeed to have such a thought of low revenge, but James erred in making this thought the precise point at which he ended his novel. The reader himself must extend his imagination to a point beyond the actual ending of the novel and realize that there is still another change in Newman, even though it is not described. The reader himself must assume that he attains a state when he will no longer have such instinctive and base thoughts. Thus at the end James had disregarded one of the aims stated in the preface written later for *The American*: "My concern, as I saw it, was to make and to keep Newman consistent; the picture of his consistency was all my undertaking. . . ."

Although many analyses of James's methods of revision have been published, including five devoted entirely to comparison of the two versions of *The American*,[1] not one of them has noted this inconsistency and James's deletion of Newman's "instinct" in the revised edition of 1907. The second version of the novel has a completely new ending. James omitted the last two paragraphs of the early version and added two and a half new paragraphs. The revised edition ends with Mrs. Tristram's expressing sympathy for Claire: " 'Ah, poor Claire!' she sighed as she went back to her place. It drew from him, while his flushed face followed her, a strange inarticulate sound, and this made her but say again: 'Yes, a thousand times—poor, poor Claire!' "

If Newman's turning toward the burned note in the first version represented a final moral struggle, James has deleted the entire struggle. Thus he has made Newman a little better but perhaps also a little less human. One could almost wish that James had written a third version which included the struggle and which also let Newman conquer his baser "instincts" permanently.

In the revised version, Newman's "inarticulate sound" and his thoughts of Claire during the last moment of the action of the novel are consistent with James's original conception of a character who "would have at the end" nothing besides "the moral

[1] Pelham Edgar, *Henry James: Man and Author* (Boston, 1927), 237–245; Royall A. Gettmann, "Henry James's Revision of *The American,*" *American Literature,* XVI (January, 1945), 279–295; Isadore Traschen, "An American in Paris," *American Literature,* XXVI (March, 1954), 67–77; Max F. Schulz, "The Bellegardes' Feud with Christopher Newman: A Study of Henry James's Revision of *The American,*" *American Literature,* XXVII (March, 1955), 42–55; Isadore Traschen, "James's Revisions of the Love Affair in *The American,*" *The New England Quarterly,* XXIX (March, 1956), 43–62.

convenience, indeed the moral necessity, of his practical, but quite unappreciated, magnanimity; and one's last view of him would be that of a strong man indifferent to his strength and too wrapped in fine, too wrapped above all in *other* and intenser, reflexions for the assertion of his 'rights.' "

If James correctly remembered his original conception of the novel after so long a time (and I think he did), he had been unable to achieve the fullest realization of his character's goodness and generosity when he wrote the original version. The character in the conclusion of the revised version has completely forgotten his instincts and the possibility of revenge. He is wrapped up in intense and fine reflections. Here, then, is evidence of maturity and superior craftsmanship at the time of the revision.

William T. Stafford

The Ending of James's *The American:* A Defense of the Early Version

Although I consider it somewhat perilous to disagree with Henry James's judgments about his own work, I cannot agree that the revised ending of *The American* is superior to the early version or that the revision itself, as Floyd C. Watkins contended in this journal, is "evidence of maturity and superior craftsmanship at the time of the revision."[1] In fact, here is one instance, in my opinion, wherein James's strategy led him woefully astray. "The free play of . . . unchallenged instinct," the phrase James later used to characterize his method at the time he wrote *The American,* a method he viewed at the time of writing the Preface with "a certain sad envy,"[2] might well, in this particular, have been the better method to have followed.

From *Nineteenth-Century Fiction,* XVIII (June, 1963), 86–89. Copyright © 1963 by The Regents of the University of California. Reprinted by permission of The Regents.
1 "Christopher Newman's Final Instinct," *NCF,* XII (June, 1957), 85–88.
2 *The Art of the Novel,* ed. R. P. Blackmur (New York, 1934), p. 25.

The first version of the novel ends with Mrs. Tristram telling Newman, after he had thrown his incriminating evidence against the Bellegardes into the fire, that they had defied his threats, not because of their innocence or "their talent for bluffing things off," but because of "their confidence" in his "remarkable good nature!" To this observation the single sentence is added: "Newman instinctively turned to see if the little paper was in fact, consumed; but there was nothing left of it." The revised version in the New York Edition ends with Mrs. Tristram telling Newman, after he had burned the paper, that " 'I needn't tell you at this hour how I've felt for you. But I like you as you are,' she said." It then continues:

> "As I am—?"
> "As you are." She stood before him and put out her hands as for his own, which he a little blankly let her take. "Just exactly as you are," she repeated. With which, bending her head, she raised his hand and very tenderly beautifully kissed it. Then, "Ah, poor Claire!" she sighed as she went back to her place. It drew from him, while his flushed face followed her, a strange inarticulate sound, and this made her but say again: "Yes, a thousand times— poor, poor Claire!"

Watkins himself avers that in the revised version James "has made Newman a little better but perhaps also a little less human." And he had previously said that it was not inconsistent for Newman "instinctively" to wish again to prove the Bellegardes wrong under the provocation of Mrs. Tristram's statement that the Bellegardes "were right." But "James erred," Watkins contends, because "the reader himself must extend his imagination to a point beyond the actual ending of the novel . . . [in order to] realize that there is still another change in Newman, even though it is not described." James changed the ending, this argument continues, to bring it more in line with the conception of the novel as stated in the Preface: "my concern . . . was to make and to keep Newman consistent; the picture of his consistency was all my undertaking. . . ."

Whatever the reason for the change, it does not thereby follow that James "had been unable to achieve the fullest realization of his character's goodness and generosity when he wrote the original version." Nor does it thereby follow that James's revised portrait of Newman is more consistent than the one in the earlier version. We know long before the final scene that Newman is not going to publish his incriminating evidence against the Bellegardes. We begin to know that he will not when Urbain de Bellegarde, in his last scene with Newman, refuses to act under the threat of Newman's intimidating threat. We know more clearly that Newman will not act when, later in England, he is described as determined to carry "out his life as he would have directed it if Madame de Cintré had been left to him—of making it a religion to do nothing she would have disliked." And when this nobility gives way, later in America, to grim satisfaction in the Bellegardes' not knowing what he is going to do, that satisfaction itself gives way as he stands, back in Paris, before the house of the Carmelites on the *Rue d'Enfer*. And it is the moment after this in the cathedral of Notre Dame that Newman, in both versions, is clearly resigned to forgetting the Bellegardes. The early version reads: ". . . Newman's last thought was that of course he would let the Bellegardes go. If he had spoken it aloud he would have said that he didn't want to hurt them. He was ashamed of having wanted to hurt them. They had hurt him, but such things were really not his game." The revised version reads substantially the same.

The destruction of the evidence in the fire at Mrs. Tristram's is thus in both versions merely the cap of a decision already clearly made. That Newman would, under the additional provocation of discovering his good nature possibly exploited, instinctively turn to the fire is, as Watkins admits, only human. The act does not necessarily mean, however, that we have to assume another change in Newman after the novel ends, even though the fact that James did make the change is possibly evidence that he thought it did.

But in terms of structure, theme, and, I think, tone, the early version is more consistent than the revised version. For example, the technique of Newman's every act beginning with his last interview with Urbain, is one of reversal. In that interview Newman expects to find the Bellegardes cowed by the letter, but Urbain is intractable. Although Newman goes to visit the fat countess, Madame d'Outreville, for the express purpose of showing her his evidence, he cannot bring himself to reveal it. His "fancy" to make "religion" out of doing nothing Claire would have disliked sours into hoping the Bellegardes will worry. He returns to Paris determined to stay "forever," only to tell Mrs. Bread, upon his return from the cathedral, that he meant stay "away" forever. To end the novel, therefore, with Newman momentarily doubting his decision (and what reader doubts that it is not momentary?) is beautifully to have capped his little pattern of reversals (but in the opposite direction) with still another one—a technique of classic comedy.

And comedy, after all, is the central achievement of *The American*, as Constance Rourke saw years ago and as Richard Poirier has more brilliantly seen recently.[3] To have as a last view of Newman (as we have in the revised version), sitting flushed and painfully inarticulate, to have Mrs. Tristram buzzing sympathetically around in sorrow for "poor, poor Claire," is, I believe, to injure seriously the comic quality in the conception of Newman that is so strongly a part of his appeal. The early version, to be sure, does end melodramatically; but melodrama is more appropriately the tool of comedy than is pathos or sentimentality. And neat, tidy sentimentality is, I am afraid, what we have in the ending of the revised version of the novel.

---

[3] See, respectively, *American Humor: A Study of the National Character* (New York, 1931), pp. 245–265, and *The Comic Sense of Henry James* (New York, 1960), pp. 49–94.

6. The Context

Cleanth Brooks

The American "Innocence": in James, Fitzgerald, and Faulkner

Whether we Americans are really innocent or whether we are not, we have had with us for a long time the notion that Americans *are* innocent and that their innocence is of a peculiar and special sort. In recent years, this notion has come in for increased attention. Americans, in their growing self-consciousness, try to analyze the ways in which their experience differs from that of Europe and the possibly different perspectives in which they are forced to see the claims of the past and the promise of the future.

A number of years ago a friend of mine told me of sitting next to Thomas Mann at a dinner in Princeton, and taking advantage of her proximity to the great man, then a recent emigré from Germany, to say to him: "Dear Dr. Mann, please get out of your head that we Americans are a young and innocent people; we are, on the contrary, an old and corrupt people." I mention the incident not in order to insist that my friend was correct or that Thomas

From *Shenandoah: The Washington and Lee University Review* XVI (Autumn, 1964), 21–37. Copyright 1964 by the author. Reprinted by permission.

Mann stood in special need of her exhortation. I make the allusion simply to indicate that there is no easy consensus on this matter of "innocence" and that the adjective can mean any of several things. But the fervor of my friend's admonition and the fact that she thought that intellectuals from Europe needed to hear it, testifies at least to the fact that the topic is a live one.

The subject is still very much alive. For example, a book review in last year's *Times Literary Supplement* begins with the statement that Americans, of course, "believe that every problem is soluble." And, having just quoted that, if I raise my eyes from my paper at this moment to look into your faces, I think that I can detect a good many that wear an expression which amounts to saying: "Yes, of course; isn't every problem soluble?" And who am I to say that perhaps you are not right? But the Englishman who wrote the review obviously did not see it as one of those self-evident truths that are implied by, if not specifically mentioned in, our Declaration of Independence. If most Americans do feel that every problem is soluble, then this fact too may have some bearing upon this matter of our innocence. So may a great many other things, including aspects of our foreign policy. But, for the purposes of this lecture, I shall respect my own limitations and confine myself to American literature. What I propose to talk about is the way in which three great American novelists have treated the "innocent" American. My texts will be Henry James's *The American*, first published in 1877, F. Scott Fitzgerald's *The Great Gatsby*, published in 1922, and William Faulkner's *Absalom, Absalom!* published in 1936. The novels themselves thus span some sixty years, and the authors may be thought to represent three rather different regional viewpoints, those of the East, the Midwest, and the South.

Henry James's story is that of an American millionaire who, at the age of thirty-five, came for the first time to Europe to amuse himself in the old world, to become acquainted with its culture, and, at the suggestion of an expatriate friend living in Paris, to seek the hand in marriage of a French noblewoman, Claire de Cintré, née Bellegarde. His intended wife is a beautiful and cultured young widow, a descendant of a family proud of its thousand-year-old history. Surprisingly enough, the American's simplicity, directness, sheer audacity—his great wealth, incidentally, is no handicap—almost succeed. But in the end, the engagement is broken. The dowager and her son find that they cannot, after all, accept the upstart American. Claire retires from the world by entering a nunnery, and the businessman prepares to come back to America.

James's hero—his name significantly is Newman—has a great deal of innocence, but it is coupled with a considerable degree of self-awareness. He has his own pride as a self-made man, but he is no vulgarian, and James expects the reader to view him with sympathy. To counterpoise his "innocence," James has made the Bellegardes—at least the mother and the elder son—definitely wicked and, as we learn at the end, they have actually committed a crime.

Fitzgerald's hero, Jay Gatsby, is like James's Newman, a self-made man. His fortune was built up rapidly during the Prohibition era, and though we are not told in detail just how it was accumulated, his financial manipulations clearly will not bear inspection. But Gatsby, though his great wealth is tainted, is in his own way an idealist—he lives for an idea—and manages to preserve a kind of innocence which, in the total context, is not simply amusing and odd, but magnificent.

Before making his fortune, Gatsby has fallen in love with a young woman named Daisy, but as a soldier preparing to be sent overseas in the first World War, a man moreover without money, he is not able to marry the girl, and Daisy lands in the arms of Tom Buchanan, an eligible suitor who has money and some kind of social position.

The chalice of love that poor deluded Gatsby—born Gatz—bears for four years, safely through the jostling throng, is his idealistic love for Daisy. It is for her that he has accumulated a fortune, and now in the monstrously big house that he has bought across the harbor from the Buchanans, he looks wistfully every night at the little green light on the Buchanan dock. Finally, Gatsby meets Daisy again and tries to reclaim her for true love. The effort fails, of course, as it must; but in contrast to the shoddy, plutocratic society which has swallowed up Daisy, Gatsby's innocence—even though we must put it very carefully within quotation marks, shines with a hard and gemlike flame—or if you prefer Shakespeare to Pater—shines 'like a good deed in a naughty world. Fitzgerald makes it quite plain that the world inhabited by the Buchanans is a naughty world.

William Faulkner's self-made man is named Thomas Sutpen. He was born in the mountains of western Virginia, but his shiftless family drifts down into the Tidewater country, and there the

young boy undergoes an experience that changes his whole life.
One day his father has him take a message to one of the planters,
and the boy, in his innocence, calls at the front door of the great
house, only to be turned away by the liveried Negro servant who
tells him to go around to the kitchen door. From this moment
onward, Sutpen's life is transformed. It now becomes of the highest
importance for him to get the means to build for himself such a
plantation house, properly equipped with liveried servants so that
he can some day open the door to the wide-eyed, ragged, proud
youngster who had been himself.

Sutpen goes to the West Indies and acquires wealth. But there
something happens which causes him to abandon his West Indies
estate and to start all over again in Faulkner's Yoknapatawpha
County. He arrives with a wagonload of wild, French-speaking
Negroes and little other than his own courage and zeal and sheer
will power. *Absalom, Absalom!* is in part the story of how Thomas
Sutpen wrests another great plantation house from the swamps
of the frontier country and finds a wife and tries to establish a
dynasty. Like Gatsby and like Christopher Newman, he has a
qualified success, though he is never able fully to realize his great
dream. Like James, Faulkner has his hero partially overcome the
resistance which the society sets up against him. Unlike Fitzgerald,
Faulkner reveals some sympathies for the values of the society
which the intruder would take by storm. Indeed, a close look at
Newman, Gatsby, and Sutpen ought to tell us a great deal about
the nature of innocence, for in spite of the differences among
these three characters, each is obviously to be regarded as in some
sense innocent. But since the nature of innocence is the problem at
issue—the matter to be defined—let us begin with more objective
matters. What are some of the common factors that all three men
share?

In the first place, all three, in effect, come out of nowhere,
their families can give them nothing and do not share their
ambitions. There is no process of nurturing, no family tradition
that is handed on. Each of our heroes leaves his family early and
strikes out on his own.

In such a situation, there is little place for formal education,
and for each of our heroes school attendance is sketchy. Christopher Newman had dropped out of school at the age of ten. When
we meet him twenty-five years later, he is so articulate and his
grasp of language is so sound that one wonders whether Henry
James has not portrayed him as a little too good to be true. But

by any standards Newman was a remarkable man, and perhaps the school of experience taught him not only how to make money but how to handle the English language.

Thomas Sutpen "had schooling during a part of one winter." But this boy of thirteen or fourteen found very quickly that the classroom was not for him, and was off to the West Indies to make his fortune. Like James, Faulkner has allowed him a formality of speech that amounts to courtliness. This rhetorical quality in his speech may be hard to account for except that, like Newman, Sutpen evidently took his self-education seriously.

Even Gatsby follows this general pattern. Fitzgerald tells us that his "parents were shiftless and unsuccessful farm people" and that the boy's "imagination had never really accepted them as his parents at all." By the time that he is seventeen, Gatsby had managed a few months' attendance at a small Lutheran college in Minnesota, but he is simply a clam digger on the shores of one of the Great Lakes when his patron-to-be discovers him and takes him up.

What is true of all of these men is not that they are all "self-made" merely in the fact that they did not inherit their wealth. In a far more important way, they are self-made—in the sense that they have created their own personalities and disciplined their minds in the service of a dream. Fitzgerald tells us that "the truth was that Jay Gatsby . . . sprang from his Platonic conception of himself." So it is with Thomas Sutpen. Sutpen once told his sole friend in the community that he knew that he possessed courage and as for the cleverness, "if it were to be learned by energy and will in the school of endeavor and experience" he would learn. Sutpen's deepest belief is that a courageous man, if he plans carefully enough, can accomplish anything.

Though Gatsby will seem, when measured against Sutpen's intensity, somewhat relaxed and offhand, his creed is much like Sutpen's. He is possessed by the same kind of devouring idealism. When Gatsby's friend tries to suggest to him that what has happened has happened, and that one simply "can't repeat the past," Gatsby cries out incredulously: "Can't repeat the past? Why, of course you can!"

Much has been made by Faulkner critics of Sutpen's inhuman "design"—his plan to set up a dynasty—a scheme to which he sacrifices everything. Because of the traumatic experience which he has suffered as a boy, he is not only obsessed by the need to achieve his dream of grandeur and success, but he has a fixation upon the specific terms of his dream of success. He must win not just any mansion, but a particular mansion. When he finds that his wife in Haiti possesses a trace of Negro blood, he abandons her and their child—not, if I read his character correctly, because he had any intense racial feeling, but because she did not fit the specific terms of the "design" that had captured his imagination. Much later, in Mississippi, when the son of that first marriage appears at his Mississippi plantation door, he refuses to acknowledge him in any way because a son with even a trace of Negro blood will not fit the details of the design that has become frozen in his imagination. Thus Sutpen sacrifices his colored son to the design, and to it he later sacrifices his two white children just as ruthlessly.

Indeed, Sutpen has not only a "design," as calls it in his conversation with General Compson, but he has also what he calls his schedule—that is, his time table—in accordance with which the design is to be realized. What he seems most to resent in the family of his Haitian wife is that their deception made him waste time—made him throw his schedule out of kilter.

Jay Gatsby, of South Dakota, lived by a schedule too. One of the most poignant things about this young gangster-idealist is a scrap of paper that turns up late in the story. After Gatsby's death, Nick Carraway comes upon a bit of paper dated September 12, 1906, bearing the word "schedule":

Rise from bed	6 a.m.
Dumbell exercise and wall-scaling	6:15-6:30
Study electricity, etc.	7:15-8:15
Work	8:30-4:30 p.m.
Baseball and sports	4:30-5:00
Practice elocution, poise and how	
to attain it	5:00-6:00
Study needed inventions	7:00-9:00

GENERAL RESOLVES

No wasting time at Shafters or [a name, indecipherable]
No more smokeing or chewing.
Bath every other day
Read one improving book or magazine per week
Save $5.00 [crossed out] $3.00 per week
Be better to Parents.

It is touching to see how this seventeen-year-old boy sought with a fierce austerity to pull himself up by his own bootstraps. But the discovery has its ominous side, for men who rule their lives in this way are likely to suffer an elephantiasis of the will. In both Thomas Sutpen and Jay Gatsby that faculty is developed to the point of deformity.

And what of Christopher Newman? Does he too live by a schedule? James has not made of Newman the extreme case that Fitzgerald and Faulkner make of their heroes, but there is enough evidence to show that all three are of the same breed. James has provided plenty of indications of Newman's own self-absorption in his design and the deliberate calculation that went into it. Here is Newman, for example, on the subject of securing a suitable wife. He tells his friend Mrs. Tristram: "I want a great woman. I stick to that. That's one thing I can treat myself to. . . . I want to possess, in a word, the best article on the market." When Mrs. Tristram reproaches him for being "so cold-blooded and calculating," her comments may, if we like, be put down to friendly banter, and when Newman calls his ideal of a wife "the best article on the market," he is quite possibly speaking tongue-in-cheek. But he is not speaking altogether tongue-in-cheek when he tells Mrs. Tristram that to win the most beautiful wife, "a man . . . needs only to use his will, and such wits as he has, and to try." This is Sutpen's formula of know-how and courage all over again.

Madame de Bellegarde, the patrician old lady who is Claire's mother, at one point remarks of her prospective son-in-law that he chooses his future wife "as if he were threading a needle," and we are at liberty to dismiss this, if we like, as the sub-acid remark of a prospective mother-in-law. But to Newman himself the thought occurs that he must seem "a trifle 'pushing.' "

At the end, when the engagement has been broken, Newman feels a sense of outrage at Claire's mother and elder brother, and acute sadness for Claire, but he is scarcely heart-broken. His dominant emotion had been "the prospective glory of possession," the possession of a creature so obviously admirable and so much admired by all the world. Romantic love, Newman had from the beginning disclaimed; as for the tenderness of a shared experience, from that, too, he was barred. In a very real sense, and not necessarily through any fault of his own, Newman had had almost no opportunity to know the woman whom he was to marry.

By contrast, Fitzgerald's Gatsby had had a passionate experi-

ence with the girl with whom he was in love. As a young army
officer in 1917, he had seemed very attractive to the eighteen-year-
old girl and there had been for a few weeks a passionate affair
which had left him feeling truly married and which had made the
girl herself resist for a time what Fitzgerald called "the pressure
of the world outside"—pressure that brought about her marriage
to another man. Daisy's friend, Jordan Baker, later tells Nick Carraway about finding Daisy just an hour before the bridal dinner
"lying on her bed as lovely as the June night in a flowered dress—
and as drunk as a monkey. She had a bottle . . . in one hand and a
letter in the other." The letter, of course was from Jay Gatsby.

The marriage arrangements made by Faulkner's hero, Thomas
Sutpen, more nearly resemble those of Christopher Newman. In
the first place, Sutpen and Newman lived in a more formal age—
Newman's courtship occurred in 1869; Sutpen's courtship and marriage in 1833. But it is principally their temperaments which
make them differ sharply from Fitzgerald's twentieth-century hero.
When Thomas Sutpen, having already made one false start in trying to realize his great design, comes into north Mississippi, this
time he chooses with very great care indeed the woman who is to
be the mistress of his manor house and mother of his children.
Many years later he was to tell General Compson: "You see, I had
a design in my mind. . . . to accomplish it I should require money,
a house, a plantation, slaves, a family—incidentally, of course, a
wife." The adverb he employs is eloquent. Sutpen does not make
his second marriage driven by some gust of passion or enamoured
of a pretty face. His wife is to be adjunctive to the design and
her place in the design is calculated to a nicety.

One might have expected Sutpen, the self-made man, who
owned nearly one hundred square miles of land, to choose a daughter of one of the plantation owners round about, into whose society
he sought to enter. But Sutpen makes his calculation in very
different terms. The frontier country was highly suspicious of this
strange intruder; his ways were not their ways. There were dark
rumors as to how he had accumulated his sudden fortune. Indeed,
soon after his entry into Yoknapatawpha County, Sutpen was
almost lynched by a group of vigilantes. Sutpen is acutely aware of
his lack of respectability. Land and wealth he has in abundance,
but respectability is harder to purchase, and Sutpen proposes to
acquire a saving measure of it quickly by marriage. He chooses,
therefore, for his wife, the daughter of the most respectable man
in Jefferson, the austere proprietor of a small store, a man who is a

Methodist steward and the principal layman in his little church.

The calculation may strike us as naive, and as not likely to achieve the desired result. But Sutpen, of course, *is* naive. After all, he is one of my three exhibits of American innocence, the kind of innocence which General Compson described as involving the belief "that the ingredients of morality were like the ingredients of pie or cake and once you had measured them and balanced them and mixed them and put them into the oven it was all finished and nothing but pie or cake could come out." Sutpen, in short, is not only a man who lives for a design and by a schedule, but a man who makes his dispositions in terms of recipes and formulas: so many ounces of respectability of prime quality will neutralize so many ounces of infamy.

After the collapse of his plans to marry Claire de Bellegarde, Newman's confidant, Mrs. Tristram, asks him: "Are you very sure that you would have been happy?" Perhaps she is simply trying to comfort him: the grapes were sour after all; yet, from what has been presented in the novel, we have no reason to think that her statement is incorrect. It is hard to believe that this admirable but ill-assorted pair would have been happy in Europe, nor can I believe that Claire de Bellegarde would have really been happy in St. Louis.

Newman sees himself as a kind of St. George sallying out of the new world to save a beautiful maiden from the clutches of an old-world dragon, but he fails in his mission. Had Jay Gatsby had better luck and rescued his maiden from her dragon, would he have been happy? Perhaps, but there is nothing in the novel to make one think so, and there are some things in it that seriously call in question any supposal that he and his dream girl—for that is literally what she is—could have lived happily ever after. It is not merely a question of Daisy's superficiality—of her initial weakness or of the corrupting influence of her life with Tom Buchanan. The most ominous portent lies in the character of Gatsby himself —in his "innocence." For Gatsby is a man in the grip of a powerful illusion and his image of Daisy surely could not have survived the flesh-and-blood experience of the actual Daisy. Fitzgerald has hinted that Gatsby himself may have sensed this possibility. Early in his courtship of Daisy, Fitzgerald tells us, Gatsby had a sort of vision: in the evening light the blocks of the sidewalk seemed to form a ladder that "mounted to a secret place above the trees— he could climb it, if he climbed alone, and once there he could suck on the pap of life, gulp down the incomparable milk of wonder."

Nevertheless, he seeks Daisy's lips and "forever wed his unutterable visions to her perishable breath."

Here it is appropriate to observe that both Newman and Gatsby dismiss the claims of family, of the past, and of society in general in favor of the intimate communion of two people who feel they need nothing for their happiness but each other. This notion, whether or not it is to be called innocent, is good American doctrine. The American snarls: "I married you, not your family." Or he sings—or sang in the '20's— "We'll build a sweet little nest / Somewhere out in the West / and let the rest of the world go by." The statistics on divorce in America would suggest that this confidence is indeed "innocent." Fitzgerald, who is not innocent in this sense, gives more than a hint that he knows how things would have gone with Daisy and Gatsby, and, as we have remarked, James is willing to have Mrs. Tristram tell Newman that he probably would not have been happy.

There is, by the way, something curiously virginal about all three men. General Compson was sure that Sutpen was a virgin until he had won and married his Haitian wife. But in any case, Sutpen never seems to be a man of sensuous indulgence. One senses that he reined in his sexual appetite with all the rigor befitting a Puritan patriarch, and that carnal knowledge for him was merely for the propagation of children. As for Newman, there is also something curiously virginal about him. We are told by the author that Newman likes the company of women, that he was not shy with them, that rather in their company he sat "grave, attentive, submissive, often silent . . . simply swimming in a sort of rapture of respect." Very frankly, I must say that this seems to me to smack of Henry James's own primness and it is not quite what we expect from a go-getting young American of thirty-five, who had lived by his wits from boyhood and had roved about the continent. Be that as it may, Newman does not seem to be a man who knows much about women and his relations with Claire de Bellegarde bear this out. He never acts like a man moved by passion, and it is fitting that his physical relations with Claire amount to no more than a single kiss, his kiss of relinquishment and farewell.

The case of Jay Gatsby is somewhat different. We are told that "He knew women early, and since they spoiled him, he became contemptuous of them, of young virgins because they were ignorant, of the others because they were hysterical about things which in his overwhelming self-absorption, he took for granted." Thus Fitzgerald has made it easier to believe in his hero; yet there is something abstemious about Gatsby after all. In the course of the gay parties given by his older patron, in which "women used to rub champagne into his hair," he "formed the habit of letting liquor alone." At his lavish parties on Long Island, Gatsby moves about with a certain genial detachment and even aloofness. If he lacks the virginal quality of Newman and Sutpen, he resembles them in his Puritanism and in his own special kind of fastidious idealism.

But what of innocence? Can Sutpen really be said to possess the innocence that is characteristic of Newman and Gatsby? Newman and even Gatsby are obviously more sinned against than sinning, and have a hurt and injury inflicted upon them which they do not deserve. Sutpen, however, inflicts injury. Yet plainly Sutpen's deficiencies in the matter of sympathy and love are finally an aspect of his defective sense of reality, and his complete self-absorption in his design is possible only to a man who is impervious to the claims of reality. Sutpen's innocence is not mere sinlessness, but an inability to comprehend what sin is.

Thomas Sutpen, as General Compson finds out to his consternation, really believes that the world is a kind of mechanism which can be manipulated if one is shrewd enough and calculates carefully enough, and that the blueprint for an action—or for a life—so calculated, can be realized provided one has the courage to see the plan through. When the child of his first marriage turns up to confront him in Mississippi, he does not feel guilty. He has not committed a sin. He has simply made a mistake—this is his own term for it—and what he wants to do is to recheck his calculations so that he can try once more and this time realize the design. As Quentin Compson tells this part of the story to his roommate, when Sutpen's son born in Haiti turns up, he is not for "calling it retribution, no sins of the father come home to roost; not even calling it bad luck, but just a mistake . . . just an old mistake in fact which a man of courage and shrewdness . . . could still combat if he could only find out what the mistake had been."

Sutpen's innocence, then, amounted to a radical defect in his perception of reality. He has an overweening confidence in his own will and in his power to calculate a course. He tells General Compson how, when he abandoned his first wife, "his conscience had bothered him somewhat at first but that he had argued calmly and logically with his conscience until it was settled. . . ." The man who can argue calmly and logically with his conscience until he settles its hash is of course capable of doing anything, but I do not mean to make fun of Sutpen. He makes this statement to General Compson in full seriousness. Perhaps his seriousness is a measure of his capacity for real inhumanity.

I suggest, then, that the monstrous inhumanity of Thomas Sutpen is an extension and specialization of certain American traits which are familiar enough and which in other contexts may even appear admirable. Newman's rather cold-blooded calculation and Jay Gatsby's confidence that one can repeat the past involve similar oversimplifications of reality.

I remarked earlier in this paper that as we compared the attitudes toward innocence of our three authors, certain regional traits might emerge. Perhaps they do. Faulkner's Southern culture, with its stubborn ties with the past, its powerful sense of the claims of family and community, and what might be called its still vital sense of original sin, may be thought to make itself felt in Faulkner's harsher treatment of innocence as compared with the treatment we find accorded by James and Fitzgerald. Thomas Sutpen is, for all of his impressive qualities, a rather obvious villain, whereas Christopher Newman and Jay Gatsby are not. Moreover, Faulkner seems to show more sympathy for the community into which Sutpen comes and with which he collides than James shows for the old-world society against which Newman pits himself, and certainly far more than Fitzgerald shows for the glittering world of money and social prestige that Jay Gatsby plans to take by storm.

This general contrast between Faulkner and the other two novelists would seem to be supported by American literary history. Other Southern writers tend to treat with a certain awe, but also a certain distrust, the new untrammelled man who has cast off the claims of the irrational past and in doing so has tapped a vast new reservoir of energy. I am thinking, for example, of such characters as Brogan Murdoch, in Robert Penn Warren's *At Heaven's Gate*, or George Posey in Allen Tate's novel, *The Fathers*. George Posey is, in personality, very different from Thomas Sutpen, but his basic role is the same: Posey seems to the young Virginian, whose sister he has married, brilliant, resourceful, and possessed of a magnetic personal charm. For his young brother-in-law he retains to the very end an attractive boyish innocence, but Tate portrays him as a violently destructive force, wreaking havoc upon the family with which he has become allied.

In this general connection, I ought to cite *The American Adam*, published some years ago, by my colleague, R. W. B. Lewis. Lewis develops in masterly fashion the special view of America that arose in the nineteenth century. The citizen of this new world, it was now proclaimed, had shaken off the evils of the past, had emancipated himself from the burden of time, and, relying upon his natural virtues, was now ready to stride confidently into a beckoning future. In short, Lewis has described, with a special emphasis upon New England, the intellectual climate that produced the self-made men who seem so characteristically "American."

Yet if one is tempted to find in Faulkner's special treatment of innocence something characteristic of his regional culture, one must be careful not to make too much of Faulkner's difference from his fellow novelists. His use of the term "innocence," for example, is not eccentric and perverse. Henry James would have understood what Faulkner meant. The evidence is to be found in James's own novels. Lewis tells us that James's treatment of the theme of innocence involved a "very long series of innocent and metaphorically new-born heroes and heroines," and he points out further that these qualities of innocence are treated by James "with every conceivable variety of ethical weight." Even in *The American* it is plain that James regards the innocence of a man like Newman as not merely, and not wholly, admirable. Lewis remarks that in his fiction James made it quite clear that "innocence could be cruel as well as vulnerable." Indeed, Lewis writes that in James's novel *The Golden Bowl* there "is a startling inversion of the Adamic tradition; it is the world, this time, which is struck down by aggressive innocence." An "aggressive innocence" that destroys the world about it approaches in character the kind of innocence that I find in Faulkner's Thomas Sutpen.

Even Fitzgerald seems to imply such a conception of innocence, for his Jay Gatsby is not the only innocent in his novel. Consider Daisy and Tom Buchanan. The term that Fitzgerald applies to them is, to be sure, not innocent but "careless." He has Nick Carraway observe that "They were careless people, Tom and Daisy—they smashed up things and creatures and then retreated back into their money or their vast carelessness. . . ." This is Nick's bitter final characterization of the pair. Nick had meant to reproach Tom Buchanan for having in effect connived at Gatsby's murder. But in his final interview with Tom, Nick tells us: "I felt suddenly as though I were talking to a child." In saying this, Nick

is indeed very close to calling Tom "innocent"—that is, a man
who has not yet found out what reality is like and who has not yet
transcended the child's self-centered world.

This discussion has seemed to imply that innocence is not a
quality wholly good or desirable; that, on the contrary, it is something to be sloughed off in process of time—a state to be grown
out of—a negative thing that ought to disappear with the acquisi-
tion of knowledge and moral discipline. I plead guilty to this
emphasis, but it does seem to be the emphasis of two, and perhaps
of all three, of the novelists we have been considering. But I am
not one to quarrel over a term as such, and I am perfectly willing
to try to conclude on a positive note—or at least with a positive
value assigned to the term "innocence."

In order to make a case for innocence as a positive virtue, I
shall appeal to one of the great poems of our century, a poem
about innocence written not by an American but by the Irishman,
William Butler Yeats. Yet I must warn you that though Yeats
celebrates innocence, his view of it will reinforce rather than contradict the views of it that we have just been examining. (But
then, of course, that is my real reason for wanting to cite the poem
at all.)

Yeats's "A Prayer for My Daughter" was written in 1919. The
occasion is a storm howling in off the Atlantic, sweeping past the
tower home near the west coast of Ireland in which Yeats was
then living. The poet's infant daughter lies asleep in her cradle,
and the father, dreading what the future may have in store for his
child, makes his prayer for gifts and qualities that shall stay her
against the destructive forces that threaten her future. Yeats
proved a true prophet: in this poem, remember that he is predict-
ing the events of the 'thirties and 'forties and 'fifties when he
writes:

> Imagining in excited reverie
> That the future years had come, dancing to a frenzied drum,
> Out of the murderous innocence of the sea.

The storm-tossed Atlantic is murderous in its destructive power,
but, ironically, innocent too, for there is no moral implication, no
choice, no sense of guilt, merely the play of natural forces.

In contrast to this murderous innocence of nature, the poet
invokes for his daughter a different kind of innocence. He hopes

that she may live sheltered from the wind like some green laurel "rooted in one dear perpetual place." He hopes that she can keep herself free from intellectual hatred and can, from the depths of her own nature, recover a "radical innocence." The contrast is between two views of the self and two contrasted views of innocence and of nature. The murderous innocence that is amoral and that is associated with the storm winds off the Atlantic is set over against a radical innocence—that is, an innocence *rooted* like the laurel tree. And nature as capricious and cruel, mere brute force, is contrasted with a human nature which is very much like the Platonic view of the soul. One may hope to find in its depths norms and archetypes of order, indeed a reflection of the divine order.

The last stanza of the poem treats all these matters in their social aspect.

> And may her bridegroom bring her to a house
> Where all's accustomed, ceremonious;
> For arrogance and hatred are the wares
> Peddled in the thoroughfares.
> How but in custom and in ceremony
> Are innocence and beauty born?
> Ceremony's a name for the rich horn,
> And custom for the spreading laurel tree.

Man lives in the society of his fellows. In terms of man's life in human society, what is the cornucopia of Greek legend—the fabled horn of plenty? What is the spreading laurel tree? Ceremony and custom, the poet boldly answers. The true dower of gifts comes from ceremony—it is not blind nature's casual bounty.

Yet we are in the habit of thinking of innocence and beauty as the gift of nature; and we commonly oppose them to custom and ceremony, for we think of custom and ceremony as tending to sophisticate, and even to corrupt. Yeats inverts these relations. Innocence and beauty, he maintains, are not the products of nature but the fruit of a disciplined life. They spring from order. They are not the chance gifts of a capricious nature. They come from nurture and tradition.

This is a surprisingly "classical" view of man to come from a poet who regarded himself as one of the last Romantics. I would claim something of this view also for Faulkner, so often celebrated as a romantically Gothic novelist, and perhaps I might claim it for our other two novelists as well. The innocence with which we are born—if we *are* born innocent—does not suffice.

Seen in this perspective, the term "self-made" itself takes on new meanings. The self-made man has, to be sure, made his fortune and may have made his "world," but can he be called truly self-made? Or at least *well made* if he is merely *self-made?* Isn't man too much a social and political animal for such self-creation to be other than fantastic? I think that our three American novelists are in agreement on this point. Fitzgerald's remark that Gatsby "sprang from his Platonic conception of himself" hangs somewhere between amused admiration and sardonic awe, and there is a like mixture of patronising tenderness and pointed irony in James's various comments on Christopher Newman. As for Faulkner: there is no question that he sees in Sutpen's innocence what Yeats called the "murderous innocence of the sea."

Date Due